LINA

UNLEASHED

A Dog's Life with a Difficult Momma

THE FIRST TWO YEARS

LINA UNLEASHED

A Dog's Life with a Difficult Momma

THE FIRST TWO YEARS

Little Big Ears (a.k.a. Lina)

—BEAVER'S POND PRESS—
Minneapolis, MN

Lina Unleashed © copyright 2017 Robin Kelleher.

All rights reserved. No part of this book may be reproduced in any form whatsoever, by photography or xerography or by any other means, by broadcast or transmission, by translation into any kind of language, nor by recording electronically or otherwise, without permission in writing from the author, except by a reviewer, who may quote brief passages in critical articles or reviews.

ISBN: 978-1-59298-823-5
Library of Congress Catalog Number: 2017906973
Printed in the United States of America
First Printing: 2017
21 20 19 18 17   5 4 3 2 1

Beaver's Pond Press, Inc.
7108 Ohms Lane
Edina, MN 55439-2129

(952) 829-8818
www.BeaversPondPress.com

To order, visit www.ItascaBooks.com or call
1-800-901-3480 ext. 118. Reseller discounts available.

All my best face licks-

Lina

For Momma, with love and boundless face licks, for doing her best to raise me and her help with *Lina Unleashed*. I am sorry that it was necessary to throw her under the bus so many times, but my story was just "begging" to be told.

Also, thanks and love to Nanny Becky and Dr. Becca for their expert care and help in guiding Momma and me through those tumultuous first two years.

INTRODUCTION

Hi! My name is Lina, pronounced with a long *i*. I am named after my grandmother once removed (from human to animal). I am a Toy Australian Shepherd. Momma wanted a "toy" dog because she thought it would be cool to carry one in her purse à la Paris Hilton, but her plans were quickly foiled—I grew like a weed.

I am from Florida, the Sunshine State. For some odd reason, Momma decided there were no acceptable dogs in Minnesota (or any states in between), so she flew to Florida to kidnap, er . . . *adopt* me, and now here I am—in the Land of 10,000 Lakes and minus-twenty-degree temps. Momma loves the water and tried to sell me on the ten thousand lakes thing and all the fun we would have, but I wasn't fooled. I know that for ten months of the year, those lakes are frozen over, and I'm not much for ice fishing or skating. Actually, I'm not much for the water at all, but that's another story.

Speaking of my momma, she's difficult. Actually, *disturbed* might be a better description, but she is an attorney, and I have to be careful what I say around her. To be honest though (and that's an absolute defense to defamation, I'm told), Momma is a bit ditzy and totally lacking in common sense—especially when it comes to caring for me. She is also socially awkward and embarrasses herself (and me) on a regular basis. In fact, I think the term faux *paw* was coined with her in mind.

Momma is also befuddled by modern technology, is a hopeless shopaholic (although she has deluded herself into thinking she's on a budget), and to top it all off, is an insufferable Republican. Life with her is challenging to say the least, and it seems we are always just a misstep away from another catastrophe.

Anyway, Momma picked me up on November 7, 2014, and we flew home the next day to Minni (as they like to call it here as if it were some kind of Disneyland) just in time for winter—great plan. Here I am wondering what has happened to me.

As you might guess, it didn't take me long to realize that life with Momma would be anything but normal. In fact, it was so fur-raising that I decided I must write about it and started linasdogblog.com.

Lina Unleashed is based on my blog and chronicles our first two years together as we navigate the often choppy waters of life (as Momma would undoubtedly put it). Yappy reading!

Me at work

Lina

WOOFDA! (I'm learning to speak Minnesotan!)

1

THE BUDGET

When I met Momma, one of the first words out of her mouth was *budget*. Seems she'd overspent and was thinking that she needed to cut back. I have since learned that Momma really can't—or won't—cut back on herself, so she must find other ways to reduce spending—like on me.

Case in point: When she picked me up in Florida, did she come with a carrier (required by the airlines), collar, leash, toy, or even a treat? She did not. I still cannot believe the breeder let me leave with her. The woman *was* concerned, though, and threw in a bag of treats and a little blanket just so I'd have something to lie on in the car for our trip to Momma's friend's place in Sarasota. By the way, shouldn't I have been restrained in the car with some kind of harness or at least been placed in the backseat to avoid an airbag injury?

I may not have made it through the trip had it not been for Momma's friend Rachel. Not only did she have dog food and water, she also had a travel carrier for my trip home to Minni! I could tell Momma was disappointed with it, though, by the way she kept looking at the carrier. It was chewed up in a few spots, and the zipper was broken. I also noticed that she pretended it wasn't hers at the Delta Sky Club at the Tampa airport, where we had to stop so she could have wine. Speaking of the Sky Club—I wonder how that fits into her budget.

Well, the term *budget* might not apply to Momma, but it sure applies to me. I am only allowed to shop at low-end pet stores and then may only buy items on clearance. You should see my coat—not only is it too big, but it is also blue. Hello! I'm a girl.

In my ratty *oversized blue* coat!

Momma *did* stop at Bone Adventure, an upscale doggie store in nearby Edina, one day to ostensibly shop for a new winter coat for me. However, she came home empty-handed—if I don't count the bags she was carrying from Nordstrom.

Momma likes to point out that she got me a new outfit for Christmas, but is a collar really an outfit? Plus, it was so small and chintzy I think it was meant for a cat. And a boy cat at that—it had a bow tie attached.

Momma says not to complain; we're going to her condo in Florida, and that can be my Christmas present. I am going to ask her to drop me off at Rachel's in Sarasota.

Lina, Looking for a Paw-out

WOOFDA!

2

MOMMA'S VILLAGE

Momma wouldn't like me saying this because she is no fan of Hillary Clinton—but apparently it *does* take a village to raise me. Let me explain.

No sooner had Momma brought me to the frozen tundra of Minnesota than she decided *she* had to return to Florida. It seems she needed to prepare for my visit to her place there and buy a few staples for me. (I still don't know why she couldn't have picked up my cheap dog crate when I came down with her after Christmas.) I also don't know how she picked up a tan if she was spending all her time getting things ready for me.

The only upside to the whole thing was that Momma hired Dr. Becca to dog sit for me. Dr. Becca is fantastic! She is an animal chiropractor and has a practice called Per**pet**ual Motion Animal Chiropractic. You can just tell by the name that she knows what she's doing when it comes to puppies (unlike some people in my life). Dr. Becca played with me, petted me and taught me new tricks. She also fed me on time and routinely took me out to go potty (and she didn't scream, "Potty!" every ten seconds like I didn't know why I was outside freezing my butt off in the sub-zero weather). Dr. Becca even did her paperwork from home one day so she could spend more time with me.

Another day, she asked my nanny, Becky (yes, I also have a nanny because I am too much for Momma to handle—even though she doesn't appear to have a job), to stop by and keep me company. By the way, I love my nanny—she's the best. Anyway, as it turns out those four days when Momma was in Florida were some of the best of my life so far.

Even in Florida, though, Momma made her presence known. One day, she sent me the following text on Dr. Becca's cell phone (and I'm quoting):

> Hi, Princess—Momma here. Are you being good? You'd better be, or you are not coming to Florida with me. I hope you are cooperating with the potty training. Remember to *only* go outside or on the training pad. Be nice to Dr. Becca, or she won't come back—and then I'm going to have to find a foster home for you. They won't care that you like pink camo coats or Bil-Jac treats. Just saying. Okay—good night now.

Luckily, Dr. Becca saw the text and assured me that she would come back and care for me anytime. However, nothing I said could convince her to cross Momma and become my foster mother.

Another person I would like to have as a foster mother is Nanny Becky. She loves me with all her heart and would do anything for me—and often has to. For example, one night I got sick in my crate and accidentally stepped in my mess. Momma found me in the morning and of course couldn't deal with the situation (I did weigh about five pounds at the time, after all), so she called Becky. Becky rushed right over and washed me in the laundry tub—it wasn't that difficult.

After my bath with Nanny Becky!

And when we finally got to Florida, Momma had no trouble enlisting help from almost perfect strangers. Would you believe she asked the construction superintendent on her building project to change my pee pad when she was out playing golf? And even though Brian has a *job*, he managed to find time to help out!

In case any of my caregivers are reading this, many thanks and a big face lick from me. And Hillary was right—it *does* take a village.

Lina, Village Dog

WOOFDA!

3

VISIT TO THE VET

You won't believe what happened today. So we went to the vet in Florida, and Momma was horrified when they weighed me and found I'd gained another pound. She knew that any hope she'd had of carrying me around like an accessory would soon be dashed. It was quite another story, however, when the doctor told her that I was overweight and that she needed to cut back on my food. Her mood brightened precipitously—she would be able to save money on my food!

Another reason Momma's mood improved was because the doctor was kinda cute. Although she tried to pretend she wasn't interested, I saw all the signs. She attempted to impress him with her knowledge of dogs and training even though I don't think she could even tell you what breed I am. She also pretended to know that dogs are supposed to get flea and heartworm medicine. She practically took over my exam from him. Next she attempted to show him her training skills by making me sit (I acted like I'd never heard the word before). Then to prove how generous she was with me, Momma asked about personal trainers, doggy day care, and overnight boarding. Finally—and this was the worst—when he showed us the boarding area, she asked if he had any private suites! As though money was no object where I was concerned!

Her little charade came to a screeching halt, though, when she went to pay. Her credit card was declined (and this after acting like she was one of the Kardashians). "There must be some mistake," Momma sniffed, demanding that they run her card again. After giving it another try, the lady announced—with some glee, I think—that the card had once again been denied. By now, we had the attention of everyone in the waiting room, and I was cowering under the counter.

Finally, Momma was reduced to writing a check so we could leave. If I'd had a tail, it would have been between my legs.

After that, Momma stopped at the Dollar Store for a little shopping—for me, of course. She wanted to buy some measuring cups to make sure I didn't get even one extra morsel of food on my new diet. She also wanted to try her credit card again—she was pretty sure that the vet's office was inept. Imagine her horror when the card was once again declined! Now she had a whole new group of spectators watching her with derision.

Luckily for me, she'd left me in the car, and luckily for her, she had a dollar in cash.

Unfortunately, we have to go back to the vet tomorrow for another shot. I'm already dreading it—she will really be "putting on the dog."

Lina, Lying Low

WOOFDA!

LIFE IN FLORIDA

Amazingly, things are going pretty smoothly in Florida. Momma is trying—but then I think I have her on the run. She is worried about all the bad publicity she has received on my blog. First she bandied about terms like *lawsuit* and *libel*. She soon dropped all the threats, however, when I informed her that my attorney, Uncle Chuck (more on him later), assured me that Momma had no claim because everything I said about her is true. Now she's resorted to bringing me the occasional gift (bribe) in hopes that her act of kindness will find its way onto my blog. Okay, she *did* buy me a little toy purse on one of her daily shopping trips to Naples.

Life is looking up in other ways, too. Momma soon discovered that if she has me with her as she wanders around the premises, there is a much greater chance that people will talk to her. So Momma goes nowhere without me now, especially if there are hunky construction workers around.

One day, the best thing happened—on one of our outings around the building, I met my saving grace—literally— Gracie Fox! She is a Cavalier King Charles Spaniel pup, and it was love at first bite with us. Here we are tussling in the grass one day:

Then, through Gracie, I met her friend, Halle, and the three of us have become fast friends—we have one or two playdates every day. Momma even managed to make friends with their mommas, Anne and Carla. Anne pays special attention to me, and sometimes we have playdates at her place when Momma is off "running errands."

Life is not without its trials, though. Every morning, after breakfast, Momma and I go for a walk. (Since I am an Aussie, Momma cleverly refers to it as a *walkabout*.) The only drawback is that a portion of Momma's preferred route includes a walk on the beach—a clear violation of local law. Momma apparently believes that the law does not apply to us, however, because she has dragged me down to the water on numerous occasions in an attempt to force me to swim (another reason she bought me was so she could use me as a prop on her paddleboard). I keep Uncle Chuck's number handy at times like this. I fear it will only be a matter of time before Momma and I are arrested.

Lina, On the Lam

WOOFDA!

Looking for cops

5

UNCLE CHUCK

Another member of Momma's village is Uncle Chuck. When Momma first got me, he was understandably concerned for my welfare, so he gave her a magazine on raising Aussies. He now provides legal services for me (pro bone-o). That might seem like an unusual need for a dog, but if you knew Momma, you'd understand. I don't think Uncle Chuck is a criminal attorney, but he knows his way around the criminal code. Also, he has connections in Florida should I need emergency help.

Speaking of connections in Florida, one day in December, Chuck texted me and told me of his plans to catch a ride from Minni to Miami on a friend's airplane. He knew that I was being held in Minni against my will, so he suggested that he bring me along! Unfortunately, though, Momma read the text, and her mind went into overdrive. She immediately hijacked (speaking of airplanes) the whole trip. First, she would be going along to "care" for me. Next came the outlandish demands like champagne and caviar. And then, to make it seem like this was all coming from me, she said to ask for Bil-Jac dog treats.

Well, as you can imagine, the whole thing backfired, and I got a stern lecture from Chuck. When I explained that Momma was pulling the strings, he got the picture. He now communicates with me only in French (he calls me Chére Niéce Lina!) to avoid Momma's prying eyes and to protect my attorney-client privilege.

"Rendez-vous a l'aeroport, l'oncle Chuck?"

Ready to leave home

Lina, Client

WOOFDA!

6

MORE VET VISITS

L ife continues to be good in Florida, with one little excep-
tion. Apparently, I ate something bad, because I ended up
with a GI problem (code for diarrhea). After a few days,
Momma announced that *she* couldn't take it anymore and made
an appointment with the vet. Clearly, she was hoping for the
handsome Dr. Garrison, but we got a wonderful young female
doc instead. I loved Dr. Megan—she was kind and gentle and
even pointed out which of my teeth were permanent and which
were still my "practice" teeth! Dr. Megan prescribed some medicine that put me on the road to recovery.

A couple of days later, though, I got sick again, and,
because it was a Sunday, Momma was forced to bring me to an

emergency animal hospital in Naples. I think the thought of the bill made Momma sick, too. Anyway, off we went. Momma was a little grumpy because this was to be her day at the pool with her friend Donna. In fact, Donna—always the adult in the room and frankly a little concerned about me—drove us there.

Things took an unexpected turn, though, when Momma saw the doctor on duty—the yummy Dr. Garny. Even *I* have to admit that he could have been one of the Chippendales.

Dr. Garny and me

(How does she find these guys? Is there a website called findhotvetsinswflorida.com?)

Anyway, as you can imagine, Momma was very helpful and cooperative, and all thoughts of the pool flew out of her head like bats out of the belfry. She was in no hurry to get home.

The doc, however, had other patients, so he promptly got down to business and looked me over. He told Momma he couldn't detect any obstruction in my bowels or other serious problem, so he would just hydrate me and give me some pain meds. When I sensed that Momma was preparing to ask for her own dose of pain meds, I pulled her out the door.

Lina, On the Road to Recovery

WOOFDA!

7

ON THE ROAD AGAIN

After finally making friends in sunny Florida and getting established in a routine there, Momma announced that we were flying home so she could go skiing in Colorado. I was horrified. I hadn't forgotten the bone-chilling weather in Minni and freezing my little (phantom) tail off while trying to go potty in a snowbank. I also did not look forward to being imprisoned in my tiny airline carrier for several hours. However, what Momma wants, Momma gets, so off we went.

Things were no different in Minni than our last stay there. We were greeting with the usual blast of arctic air and a temperature of negative eleven the night we arrived. My dread of the entire visit soon turned to joy, however, when I learned that

Dr. Becca and Nanny Becky would care for me in Momma's absence. Also, Momma finally broke down and purchased a new pink coat for me. (I'm thinking she was getting a little nervous about my next blog post—and with good reason, I might add.)

In any case, things were looking up. Momma wrote detailed instructions for Dr. Becca regarding my care, just as a normal dog owner would. First on the list was the amount of food I should be allotted each day, including the proportion of wet to dry. She also instructed that I could have treats "from time to time" if I was good.

My time with Dr. Becca and Becky was fantastic. They played with me, trained me and treated me. Dr. Becca took me with her to work one day at Per**pet**ual Motion, and I had a blast with the other animals. When I was at home during the day, Becky would stop by and play with me and take me out to go potty.

Things were going really well for everyone until, not sur-prisingly, Dr. Becca discovered that Momma hadn't left enough dry food for me. When Dr. Becca finally reached Momma in Vail on Tuesday (she was busy with après ski), her first reaction was: Couldn't we ration it out a little to make the food last until Friday when she got home? Dr. Becca patiently explained to Momma that she could not and asked what kind of dog food I ate. Of course, Momma did not know, but she rattled off some well-known brands, such as Purina, just to get off the hook.

Luckily, Dr. Becca knew of a good pet store nearby, so we drove over and found some appropriate, healthy puppy food.

I did have a moment of panic, however, when some employees decided to weigh me for the fun of it. I hadn't forgotten Momma's warning that she didn't want me to get too big, and I was afraid of further cutbacks in food. (This will explain the look of concern on my face as I'm looking at the readout on the scale.) Don't tell Momma that I am now up to nine pounds!

Me being weighed!

Lina, Pretty in Pink

WOOFDA!

MOMMA'S NEW MISSION

We are in Minni again. This time, Momma needed to get home to prepare for a trip to Europe (as I may have mentioned, the budget only applies to me). Nothing has changed here—this time we arrived to find nine inches of new snow. I really had no choice but to sit in the snow and go potty. And once again I was stuck in my tiny airline carrier and stuffed under the seat in front of Momma—for which the airline charges $125 each way.

It probably goes without saying that this has become a real *bone* of contention with Momma, especially since someone told her that human babies under a certain age fly free. Consequently, Momma has started complaining about this policy to anyone who will listen—friends, foes, neighbors, people she doesn't even know.

A few days before we left for Minni, Momma was at a brunch and brought up her new favorite subject. One of her friends told her that it was not a problem—all Momma had to do was get a doctor's excuse saying she is depressed or anxious (no problem there) and I could fly for free as a service dog! Momma was all ears—a comment she often makes about me.

A couple of days later, Momma and I came hurtling into the Fort Myers airport to fly home—running late as usual, me bouncing around amid a mountain of bags in the backseat, Momma half-crazed. She lassoed a skycap into helping us and once again launched into her usual tirade about the price of my "ticket." After taking one look at Momma, the skycap advised her—make that encouraged her—to see a mental health professional who would provide her with a note so I could fly free. That was all she had to hear—she is now hell-bent on seeing a shrink and getting that statement. (For my part, for once I am all for her little scheme—I have heard that service dogs don't have to be confined to a carrier!)

I have little doubt that Momma will be able to get herself declared crazy. And I'm looking forward to my new job—and the view from forty thousand feet.

Lina, ESA (Emotional Support Animal)

WOOFDA!

THE ATTRACTIVE NUISANCE

ast time Momma took me to the vet in Minni, it was to
have me spayed. It was a horrible experience, and I hated
it. That is why, when we went zooming back to the clinic
the other day, I was shaking like a leaf. And it turns out my fear
was well founded.

Earlier in the day, Momma decided to remove the gate
on the steps that prevented me from going upstairs. She
had been concerned that if I, for some reason, took a flying
leap between the railings to the main level, she would have
to scrape me off the floor. Now, however, she was tired of
stepping over the gate and decided to throw caution to the
wind.

All was going well—I didn't even consider playing Wonder Woman—and I had a good time exploring. Nanny Becky was over, and I enjoyed following her around while she worked and Momma read the paper. It turned out, however, that height wasn't the main danger on the second floor—there was a toxic houseplant sitting in plain view and at the perfect level for me to eat (I guess Momma had never heard of "puppy proofing" a home).

When Momma finally pulled herself away from the paper to see what I was up to, she discovered me surrounded by little green leaves from her umbrella plant and licking my lips. Amazingly, she realized that the plant I had ingested might be poisonous. This disruption in her day did not sit well with Momma because she was now pretty sure that she would not make her luncheon date downtown. She was also pretty sure there would be another vet bill involved. In fact, she specifically pointed that out to me later.

Weighing her options—my passing away versus the vet bill—Momma finally decided to do the right thing and call the clinic (plus Becky told her to). They said to either make me throw up at home or to bring me in. She lacked the skill or the supplies or the fortitude (or all of the above) to make me throw up and was also concerned about the mess, so off we went. Luckily, Becky rode along, as usual the voice of reason and calm.

I was immediately brought into the examining room at the clinic, as time was of the essence. Also of the essence was making me puke, which I did—six or seven times. As I said, my dread of the veterinary clinic was warranted. My vomit included dog food, some red string and—sure enough—green leaves! Momma barely noticed—her attention was on the bill for $87.59.

When I texted Uncle Chuck to see if I had a claim against Momma for negligence, he said that he was exploring a legal theory called the "attractive nuisance." I wonder if he was talking about the plant.

Lina, Possible Plaintiff

WOOFDA!

10

MOMMA GOES TO A TWINS GAME

The other day, Momma was invited to a Minnesota Twins game at Target Field. She was quite excited! She eagerly looked forward to experiencing the cool new stadium and the old-fashioned fun of the ball game! She was in a magnanimous mood and even gave me extra treats before she left.

When she came home, however, Momma was upset. She said it wasn't that the Tigers beat the Twins but that she wasn't happy with her experience at the game. In fact, she had the distinct feeling that the world as she knew it was over. Momma said that this was no longer a country she recognized.

It started with the wait for her host outside the stadium by the big bronze glove. She was enjoying the sunshine and the activity when suddenly the fake-cheery, yet authoritative voice of the announcer came over the loudspeaker with his pre-game remarks. He started off on a positive note with, "Welcome to Target Field," but things went downhill from there as he launched into several minutes of annoying lecturing regarding security and rules of behavior. Momma knew that rules relating to security were necessary these days (for example—no bags larger than 16"×16"×8" were permitted), but she was outraged with rules designed to make sure that no one ever did anything that could possibly offend anyone. In her opinion, his announcements sucked all the fun right out of the game.

After the obligatory announcements about bag sizes and inspections, he continued that there would be no smoking in the stadium, there was no designated smoking area, and if anyone left the ballpark (presumably to have a cigarette), there was no reentry! He also warned against using umbrellas in the event of rain, as they blocked the view of other fans. (This caused Momma to wonder when one *could* use an umbrella.) On and on the announcer went: there would be no walking in the aisles during at-bats and no signs allowed with offensive language or that hindered the views of others.

I think what finally drove her to the brink, though, was when, in the middle of the game, she spotted a message on the giant screen stating something like, "If you witness any inappropriate behavior, please report it immediately by texting the following number . . ." *Really?* thought Momma. What if she saw someone picking his nose? Or using an umbrella? Should she text?

Momma's mood was darkening. This was not the ball game experience she remembered when she saw the pennant-winning

Twins play at Metropolitan Stadium in 1965. Then, she told me, the only thing you had to worry about was whether the Twins would win and remembering the words to "Take Me Out to the Ball Game" during the seventh-inning stretch! People didn't need rules then, she fumed—they *knew* how to act. And if they did do something wrong or offensive, it was no big deal. People dealt with it—it was part of life!

Things were to get worse for Momma that day when, later in the game, she headed for the restroom. She had a cup with her to dispose of (no doubt it was a beer cup), but she couldn't figure out which trash bin to throw it in. The bin in the restroom virtually screamed PAPER TOWELS ONLY!

She was at a loss over what to do, so she carried the cup out into the concession area to find a container in which she could deposit regular trash. However, to her horror, Momma was foiled again. Every bin she saw dictated that only *organic* or *recyclable* items could be disposed of there (and she didn't know if her garbage qualified as either).

Now Momma was really rattled and noticed that people were beginning to look at her with suspicion. Scared that someone might text the number for inappropriate behavior, she stuffed the cup into her (not bigger than 16"×16"×8") bag and went home.

Sensing that her baseball game experience wasn't a home run (I'm a trained support animal, after all), I licked her face, and all was well.

Lina, ESA

WOOFDA! (Go, Twins!)

11

IT'S ALL ABOUT THAT LAKE

Ever since Momma got me, most of our activities have been geared toward making me a water dog. She wants me to swim and also to ride with her on the paddleboard and kayak. I don't know why that is so important to her, but I think it's so other boaters will talk to us.

To that end, Momma often dragged me (illegally) down to the roaring Gulf of Mexico in Florida to acclimate me to the sea. To no avail, however; it was so humongous and loud that it terrified me! She and a friend also took me to a doggie water park in Bonita Beach, where I was nearly trampled by a giant dog. Needless to say, this did not help in Momma's crusade to make me swim.

Undaunted, Momma started a new regimen when we got home to Minni. As soon as the ice was off the lake, she led me down to the shore and started throwing out little sticks for me to retrieve. I ventured out a little way—but I had my limits—the water was freezing!

Yesterday was a new chapter in our lake life. Rachel brought her dog, CoCoa, over for a backyard playdate—which was, by the way, super fun. Momma even brought out a couple of toys, including a ball and water Frisbee. Soon she was throwing the ball toward the lake, hoping to lure me into the water. I'm no fool, though, and I refused to chase it. After one errant toss, the ball went into the lake and floated beyond Momma's reach. Momma (who wouldn't dream of wading into the ice-cold water herself) was forced to grab a paddleboard and rescue the ball. As she paddled out, she pointed out that the ball had cost her $20. She also pointed out (and I quote), "If you were any kind of dog at all, you would have retrieved the ball!"

Wearing the dreaded life jacket

Even with her big push to get me wet, until now, Momma had not forced me to go out on the lake on one of her questionable vessels. All that changed yesterday, however, with the arrival of my life jacket in the mail. Our maiden voyage will be this weekend. I hope Momma will have both oars in the water.

Lina, First Mate

WOOFDA! (Batten down the hatches!)

12

ALL PAWS ON DECK

Well, Momma finally got her way. I have now been a (reluctant) passenger on both her kayak and stand-up paddleboard (SUP).

Credit to neighbor Cindy for the SUP photo on the next page. Momma spotted her boating and taking family photos and *barged* right in.

Note that I have a look of extreme concern on my squinty little face (she keeps promising me Doggles—doggie sunglasses—but must be waiting for the fall sale).

Momma's plan to get to know people on the lake with me along has been met with limited success. (I don't know when she'll realize that most people just don't view a boat ride as a chance to visit with her.) In fact, fishermen—who want it quiet—usually ignore Momma in an effort to shut her up when she calls out, "How's fishing?" One of them did put a scare into her the other day, however, when he informed Momma that she'd better watch out so a big muskie didn't get me. I, on the other paw, was somewhat relieved—maybe I wouldn't have to go in the water after all!

Last week, I had another playdate with CoCoa. Despite gale-force winds, Momma was determined to paddleboard over (we *could* have walked—Rachel only lives a block away) and announced, "We are going by sea!" Momma used me as ballast on the front of the board, which was tough duty because the waves kept crashing over me. When we somehow blew ashore at Rachel's about an hour later, CoCoa was waiting! We had a great time chasing each other around and eating dead fish.

Soon though, it was time to go home, and Momma, still in full nautical mode, proclaimed (as though she were the ancient mariner), "Time to set sail, Lina!" The wind had calmed considerably, there were no other boaters around to make fun of us, and we made it home above board. Don't tell Momma, but I could get used to this!

Lina, Padidog

WOOFDA! *(Hey, bro, SUP?)*

13

RUFF WATERS

I t has been a tumultuous week with Momma. It started with her getting a bad cold—I'm thinking it was from our rocky ride to Rachel's on the SUP. I also got sick and threw up in my crate (I think it was from some bad dog food Momma fed me—but I have to be careful about my allegations against her). Unfortunately, some of my stuffed toys in the crate were ruined, so Momma was forced to go to the pet store to get some replacements.

Do you see how she is trying to indoctrinate me at every turn? I can just sense her thinking, *You* will *learn to swim and you* will *be a Republican*. Also, do you see the clearance tags?

Momma was ostensibly too sick to do anything with me last weekend, so Rachel said she would bring CoCoa over to play with me in the backyard. Talk about a silver lining! And guess what? Without any pushing from Momma, I was able to dog paddle! Momma, of course, was watching from the window and finally couldn't stand it anymore. She miraculously overcame her illness and rushed outside to take photos—and control.

Later that week, Momma and a group of ladies—and CoCoa!— went out pontooning. We had a grand time. The ladies had coffee and breakfast, and CoCoa and I had doggie snacks and water that Rachel brought. All was going well until a huge bald eagle (known to snatch up small animals) appeared over the pontoon and began scoping us out. Momma freaked, wrapped me in her arms and yelled, "Take CoCoa! Take CoCoa!" (Okay, I made that part up cuz I saw it in a movie once, but I know she was thinking it!)

The week ended with a scorcher. We have been living without AC ever since Momma learned the cost of a new unit. First she got a price from "BigCo," but she ruled them out as scammers (they were the ones who said she needed a new one). Next she got a local guy from "SmallCo" to come out, thinking she might bully him into a good deal. However, that didn't work out either, and he left after about fifteen minutes of Momma telling him how to diagnose the problem. Afterward, Momma—who finally noticed I was panting and my eyes were glazed over—informed me, "Don't worry, Lina, we can always cool off in the lake."

I, for one, am glad that last week is over.

Lina, "Hot Dog"

WOOFDA!

DOG DAYS OF SUMMER

As they say in good old Minni, the dog days of summer are upon us. (I told Momma that phrase sounds a little doggist to me and that I'm offended, but she told me to get over it.) In any case, it's hot, and we are still lacking an air conditioner.

The big news of the day? The Doggles finally arrived! Momma was so excited, she was beside herself—she couldn't wait for me to try them out. Here I am showing her what I think of them.

Momma persevered, though, and proudly placed me on her SUP. As you can probably tell, I am looking around for help.

SOS!

As cautious as I still am about the water (it didn't help that Momma "accidentally" dunked my head in the lake the other day), I enjoy my playdates with CoCoa. Here we are glued to the action as Rachel learns to paddleboard. I am, of course, the one wearing the dorky life jacket.

The other big news of the day? We are going on a little trip to northern Minnesota—or as Momma cleverly puts it, to "upstate" Minnesota—this week! Momma tells me it is beautiful up there and that it's where she grew up (*grew up*?).

I think I'd be a little more excited about the trip if we weren't headed for another lake (with ten thousand–plus, there apparently is no escaping them in this state), and that means the water dog immersion program will continue.

The other concern is that the cabin is practically in Canada, and I'll be confined to my little doggie seat for over five hours. Momma says not to worry, however—the time will go by fast because we'll be listening to conservative talk radio the entire way.

I showed her what I thought about that and chewed up her favorite elephant pillow!

Lina, Dissident

WOOFDA!

15

UP NORTH

I had heard a lot about "Up North" from Momma prior to our trip. It was, after all, where she was raised. I know that this part of the state is near and dear to her heart. She grew up on a farm outside the minuscule town of Gully and attended school there and in nearby Gonvick. She still has many relatives and friends there and often stays at the cabin in the summer. (Forget the winter, Momma says—it's too cold. Then she snidely adds that she is still waiting for global warming to reach northern Minnesota.) I always know where Momma stands on the issues.

I also know that no one had better make derisive comments about where she grew up. For example, last winter a "friend" made a sarcastic remark about the area, saying something like "all the people up there are so *Duck Dynasty*." Well, that got Momma going because she knew the "friend" was being derogatory. Her rage was tempered, however, by the fact that she admires much about the *Duck* crew and therefore chose to take it as a compliment.

I got to experience "Up North" first paw this month when Momma and I spent ten days there. Contrary to the opinion of the uninformed, I loved it (maybe I'm a little *Dog Dynasty* myself—despite my leftist leanings!). There were people and dogs everywhere, and I got away with a lot more than when it's just Momma and me.

Her relatives really know how to push her buttons and constantly tease and make fun of her (which may explain why she is the way she is). However, they also like to tease me—do I *look* like a fish?

Since Momma was always running off to play golf in nearby Bemidji, I was often left in the care of the aforementioned relatives. In fact, I think Momma viewed her family as built-in dog sitters. They got back at her, though, sending texts like "Lina sure likes hot dogs" (off limits) and "Into the beer again; Lina is stumbling around a bit" (off limits to *me*). I know these texts drove Momma crazy (craz*ier*), but apparently not enough that she came home to rescue me.

Even after the relatives left, she relied on her "village" for my care. One day, Momma left me with some women next door who had started the day with a Bloody Mary bar. You might say that was a little negligent on her part, but I say, party! When Momma came home, she found us on the floor of their cabin—the ladies teaching me to dance on my hind legs! I'm sure Momma was a touch upset and wondered what else went on, but I wasn't about to tell her—after all, what happens at the lake stays at the lake.

Of course, the water dog indoctrination program continued unabated up there. To that end, Momma decided that a ride behind the pontoon on "Big Mable" was in order, and she put the dreaded life jacket and Doggles on me. This, needless to say, was met with whoops and hollers (think *Duck Dynasty* again) and much ridicule. Momma ignored the jabs, though, and demanded a turn on Mable—cutting short the ride of the children in front of us who actually *wanted* a turn.

On Big Mable with Jenny and Momma

Unfortunately, like all good things, our time at the cabin came to an end, and Momma announced that it was time to return to "The Cities." She had business to take care of there, she said, and errands to run (code for facials and shopping and the like). She promised we'd be coming back soon, though, and I can't wait. "Up North" is a special place, and I dare anyone to say otherwise!

Lina, Honorary Dog/Duck Dynasty Member

WOOFDA!

16

THE BIRTHDAY PARTY

I will soon be one year old (!), and plans are now in full swing for a blowout bash to celebrate my birthday. I was kind of excited at first because at least two of my doggie friends will be there, including one of my BFFs (best furry friends), CoCoa. However, as with most things Momma, the party is spiraling out of control. I don't think it's so much that Momma wants to celebrate my birthday as it is that she views the party as a chance to promote my blog. In fact, I'm pretty sure she is trying to find a way to make me pay for my keep.

Let me explain. Momma has been reading up on blogging and has learned that, as a general rule, companies will not advertise on a site unless it has about ten thousand visits per month (and that leaves us about 9,999 short). Undaunted, Momma has begun a new campaign to increase my readership—beginning with the party.

Thus, the first step Momma took to prepare was to order business cards for me (she even popped for expedited delivery so we'd get them in time). These she plans to shamelessly pass out at the party and "hound" people to spread the word!

Momma has been gearing up in other ways, too. First, she went to a party store to find hats for the dog attendees. Luckily, there were none there or at any other store she visited. She did, however, manage to dig up some doggie scarfs that my friends would be required to wear.

Next, Momma got the idea—to showcase me even more—that I should wear a little crown or tiara for the party. That also didn't go well. She did find some mini-tiaras attached to little combs at her favorite discount store, but, thank God, she could not make them stay in my hair—I mean *fur*! Unfortunately though, she did find a frilly little pink dress for me sporting the lame message IT'S MY BARKDAY!

I'm actually thinking about becoming a boy (I mostly identify as one, anyway, with the blue coat and all) so I won't have to wear it.

Despite her springing for this party, Momma hasn't forgotten how to cut corners for my care. The other day, she announced that because there's nothing in the budget for spiffing me up at a salon, she will groom me herself—this means running a brush through my fur—for the big day. In fact, the last time I was at a groomer, it was to have my nails cut. They hadn't been done in like forever, and Momma suddenly remembered she wasn't the only one who needed nail care. In a panic, she whipped me over to the neighborhood groomer—scared to death that they would turn her into PETA or the ASPCA or (as she viewed it) one of those meddling organizations.

Of course, Momma's party plans did not include any kind of food preparation. (That would cut into her own professional grooming time.) Luckily, Nanny Becky realized this omission and asked if she could provide treats for the dogs and cupcakes for the humans. When it finally hit Momma that this would not be enough food—unless the humans could be convinced to eat dog food—she called her caterer friend, Gloria, who agreed (on about a moment's notice) to help us out. Gloria even came up with a theme—Mexican Fiesta! This made Momma happy because then she could claim she contributed to the meal—even *she* knows how to make margaritas!

Stay tuned . . .

Lina, Businesswoman and Party Girl (Boy?)

WOOFDA!

17

APRÉS PARTY

I t is now the morning after, and Momma is moving a little slowly. She is bleary-eyed, sitting at the kitchen counter and staring at a mountain of doggie toys, treats, cards and doggie decor items. She, of course, has no idea who gave me what. This is going to make writing the thank-you notes difficult, if not impossible. This is Momma's own fault, by the way—she had strongly hinted that gifts were welcome (almost expected).

Despite the gift follow-up fiasco in the making, though, the party itself was a hoot! The cake and treats from Nanny Becky were delicious, and for once Momma wasn't scrimping on my food.

We had a big crowd; many of Momma's friends were there, and they were all super nice! They were fun and even helped wait on others and clean up while Momma socialized. Some of my furry friends joined us, too!

We had a blast chasing toys and each other, swimming, snacking, and generally keeping our parents on their paws, er . . . *toes*! Actually, I didn't swim except when Momma plopped me in the water next to Charlie. Momma had noticed that I was crazy about him and thought that puppy love might *Trump* (as she liked to think of it) my aversion to water, but she was wrong. I *did* spend most of the day chasing Charlie on land, however, even though he wanted nothing to do with me. (Don't tell Momma, but I overheard a friend say, "Like mother, like daughter.") Ouch!

I'm not giving up on Charlie!

After the guests had enjoyed Gloria's wonderful Mexican food, Momma announced that everyone should gather around the patio table for a gift-opening ceremony. At this point, several people rolled their eyes and muttered, "Ceremony?" I know, right?

Oblivious to the guests' growing impatience, Momma began by leading the group in a rousing rendition of "Happy Birthday" and proceeded with her endless opening of my gifts and cards, replete with a rambling explanation for each.

After the gift opening, and before she totally lost the group's attention, Momma turned to the promotion of my blog—this was the point of the party, after all. While passing out my business cards ("Take a few and give them to your friends," she insisted), Momma urged everyone to stay up to date on Lina's Dog Blog.

Last, and as proof that I'm worth reading, Momma proudly announced that I had won the 2015 "Pawlitzer Prize" for my blog. The award was presented to me by my legal counsel, Uncle Chuck, and his dog, Willie.

Everyone clapped their hands *paw*litely, but I'm not sure that we gained any readers. In fact, it seemed to have the opposite effect—as soon as Momma's little production was over, people couldn't wait to hightail it to their cars.

Back to the morning after . . . Momma is now contemplating the "A Little Hair of the Dog Cures All" message on one of the wine gift bags. It's going to be a long day.

Just remember, if you receive a thank-you note and it has nothing at all to do with the gift you gave, Momma means well. Keeping that in mind, I would like to personally woof out a big thank-you to everyone—the gifts were super cool and the party was wonderful. My tail, if I had one, would be wagging!

Lina, Little Big Girl Now

WOOFDA!

18

#ONTHEROADAGAIN

No sooner had we gotten over the hubbub of my self-serving birthday party when we hit the road again for another trip "Up North." This time, we were accompanied by the daughters of one of Momma's ex-husbands—Tammy and Talla. As usual with Momma's friends and relatives, they took over my care for the trip.

Momma was happy the girls came along because it gave her a chance to pick their brains (and not just about their father's love life). She wanted them to explain to her what *hashtag* meant. That was all she ever heard or read about these days. Hashtag this, hashtag that. Scared of being left behind, Momma wanted to learn what it was all about so she could stay relevant—and, one presumes, sound cool.

After a futile attempt to explain it to her, the girls finally gave up. Momma's eyes were glazed over, and she still didn't know the difference between a hashtag and a dog tag. Nevertheless, *hashtag* stuck in her brain, and she couldn't stop saying it. Every. Sentence. Began. With. Hashtag. Like #canyoudrivealittlefaster, #Linaneedstogopotty, and #didwebringwine. I don't know who was happiest when we finally arrived at the cabin, #butIthinkitwasme.

Just like last time, I had a blast Up North and Tammy and Talla were great. They extricated me from my crate in the morning and took me out to go potty while Momma slept in. (Momma wouldn't let them feed me, though, because she is strictly monitoring my food ever since I had an extra treat at my party.) (#youareonadiet.)

Tammy and Talla also thought up neat things for me to do with them—and they could make anything fun. For example, one day, we played canoe with an old dead tree that had blown down. I'm just surprised Momma didn't make us put it in the lake.

The only downside to our trip was the weather. It was about one hundred degrees every day with no breeze. It was so hot, I actually went in the lake on my own free will. I thought this was a great example of global warming, but I didn't dare say that to Momma. I know that I would get her standard response: "It's called *weather*, Lina."

Even though Momma doesn't subscribe to the global warming theory, she does like to point out how "green" we are because we cool off in the lake rather than in air conditioning (basically because we don't *have* air conditioning at the cabin, but don't bother Momma with the facts).

Despite the blistering heat, Momma insisted that we have a fire every day (#letsbuildafire); she said it was tradition, and plus, we could make s'mores later! So we all pitched in and built fires, raising the temperature in the yard by at least ten degrees.

Here I am trying to put out the fire and lying under the glider, glued to the cool earth and trying to get some relief from the heat.

I think everyone was relieved when it was time to go home. Momma seemed to forget all about being "green" and turned on the AC full blast! I definitely know who was happiest to be on the road again. #itwasme!

@Lina, (Hashtag) Happy Hound

WOOFDA!

19

TRYING TO TURN THE PAGE

As summer winds down and Momma's outdoor activities cur*tail*, she has decided that it is time to step up our efforts to bring my blog to the next level. She still views it as a vehicle to pay for her dog-related expenses (limited as they are). Consequently, she decided we must *bone* up on how to modernize the site and get more publicity. And she knew just the book to help us with our strategy—*Blogging for Dummies*. ("I know it's beneath us, Lina, but desperate times call for desperate measures.")

When the book arrived, Momma flipped through the table of contents, trying to pick out the parts on which we should focus. She quickly decided to skip many topics such as "Setting

Up Your Blog" and "Creating Great Content" since in her mind we had mastered them already. *This is going to be a breeze,* she thought. Maybe she would even help me write a book called *Blogging for Smarties!*

Doing some preliminary research

She soon hit a snag, though, when she came across chapters with words she didn't understand like *Tumblr, Squarespace,* and *Vlogging.* Maybe we *didn't* know everything there was to know about blogging just yet. Momma was in a hurry to get to the part of the book on making money, though, so she decided to skip some of the more technical chapters for now.

Next, she came upon the part of the book on marketing and promoting. This was *it,* she thought—this would be the key to instant success! She soon reached another dead end, though, when she read that marketing involved more things she knew nothing about—like RSS and Twitterverse. *How could this book be for dummies?*

Skipping ahead again (she really had no choice), Momma finally hit pay dirt when she got to the section called "Getting Paid to Post." *Now we're cooking*, she thought. Her excitement was short-lived, however, when she saw that she would have to read about one hundred pages and research new terms and sites like MediaWhiz and SiteScout. And there was that term again—*RSS!* Oh, and *paw*dcasting, er . . . podcasting. At this point, Momma knew she was *licked* and put the book away.

So that's where we stand at the time this goes to press— still stuck in the Stone Age. In the meantime, I hope you will spread the word about my blog—and keep your paws crossed that someday someone will miraculously decide to buy some ad space from us.

Lina, Research Assistant

WOOFDA!

20

MOMMA'S BIRTHDAY WEEKEND

Momma had a birthday recently, too, but unlike mine, she wanted to keep hers under wraps. Therefore, she won't be happy to read about it on my blog, but it *is* my blog, after all, and I retain complete editorial control. And as much as she doesn't like big government or entitlement programs, trust me, she is happy with her new medical benefits.

Momma did not spend her birthday with me. She told me she must drive up to Bemidji for business meetings on the weekend. Frankly, that was okay with me because Dr. Becca came to stay. Nanny Becky also came by and played with me when she could. So all in all, it was a nice weekend—and frankly good to have a little adult supervision for a change (did I just woof that?)!

Momma wanted to be sure that she had her ducks in a row before she left this time because, as she put it, she did not need any more bad press from me. I'm pretty sure she was thinking about the time Dr. Becca stayed and Momma forgot to leave dog food. But I *dogress.*

Momma really tried hard this time. She made sure I had food, water, and a bed, and she even gave me a little two-calorie treat before she left. I was proud of her—it seemed she had actually become a responsible dog owner. It soon became apparent that she was not quite there, however, when Dr. Becca discovered that Momma had locked her out of the house. (If I had to guess, I'd woof that Momma got a little distracted toward the end because of all the outfits she was trying on for her "meetings.")

Anyway, as usual, Nanny Becky came to the rescue, and the weekend proceeded swimmingly. Nanny and Uncle Tom came over and played with me and brought me a cupcake in honor of Momma's birthday.

Dr. Becca spent quality time with me, too—we did some training, and she took me for walks. When Momma complained to Dr. Becca that I had not been minding her on walks, Dr. Becca calmly pointed out that treats work better than threats. She also told Momma that she would go to the dog supply store before her next visit and get me a harness that fit. (Ouch!) Dr. Becca also made a special birthday card from me to Momma.

When Momma came home from Bemidji, she spent all evening on the computer. It seems she had gotten some birthday messages on Facebook and didn't know how to respond. For example, was she expected or even *able* to respond? What if she said the same thank-you message to everyone? Would her well-wishers think she was thoughtless and be offended? What if she said something personal to one person—would everyone be able to read it?

The issue only intensified when she switched between devices and email accounts. She soon forgot who she had (possibly) responded to and was now worried that she was responding twice—and if it showed up on Facebook, she would be a laughingstock. And of course she didn't know what showed up on Facebook because she did not know how to navigate the site. What was the difference between a status update, a wall and a timeline?

In the event you were one of the people who sent her a birthday greeting and didn't hear back from her—or heard back more than once—please forgive her and accept this as a personal heartfelt thank-you from Momma. I know she appreciated it!

Lina, Damage Control Specialist and Editor in Chief

WOOFDA!

21

MOMMA'S TRICKLE-DOWN ECONOMICS

As you might expect, Momma is a big proponent of the trickle-down theory of economics, where all the money starts at the top and allegedly trickles down to the little guy. As you also might expect, Momma doesn't always practice what she preaches—the only thing that trickles down at our house are spending cuts.

Arguably, the best example of her version of the trickle-down (to dog) theory was when I got stung on my paw by what I can only assume was a bee. We were at the end of the driveway retrieving the mail when the sting occurred. It hurt like heck, and I immediately let out a little yelp and started hopping around, signaling my distress to Momma. She paid little attention at first, though, engrossed as she was with her daily stack of catalogs from Nordstrom and Neiman. Finally, though, she couldn't help but notice that I was only walking on three legs.

Grudgingly (*"Now* what, Lina?"), Momma did a little exam of the injured paw and saw that it was bright pink and two of the pads were quite swollen. Not knowing anything about insect stings, especially on dogs, Momma was once again forced to call the vet's office. (What if she did nothing and I died? How would she explain that to her friends?) The nice young technician who answered the phone suggested that Momma bring me in.

When we pulled up a few minutes later, Momma examined my paw again in the car and saw that it was looking much better. At that point, she almost bolted, but then she had a better idea—she would ask the tech to take a quick (free) look to confirm but avoid the vet and his fee. Amazingly, the tech agreed, said the paw looked good, and we were on our way—Momma breezily calling out, "No charge, right?" as she whisked me out the door. I only hope we have no reason to return anytime soon.

Momma's stinginess is not strictly limited to the vet, of course. One of my favorite gifts from the infamous birthday party was a gift certificate from Nanny Becky for our neighborhood pet salon. Nanny thought it was about time that I got a nice shampoo and blow-dry. Momma immediately nixed the idea, though, informing me that Nanny would continue to give me my baths in the laundry room sink (so much for benefits trickling down to the little guy).

She said that the certificate would be used only for the occasional—my guess would be annual—nail clipping. As a result, I have been reduced to "paw tucking" until Momma can squeeze in an appointment for *my* nails.

One area in which Momma doesn't scrimp is on my "calming aid" treats. Nanny had suggested them to help with anxiety during thunderstorms and the like. What Nanny didn't realize (but frankly should have) was that Momma would use them to drug me whenever she wanted a little free time. And judging by the number we go through, I'm pretty sure the aids do not all trickle down to me.

Lina, Fur a New Deal

WOOFDA!

Paw Script: Yesterday, Momma got a card in the mail reminding her that I am due for my Bordetella shot and wellness examination. She has already determined that:

A) I do not need the shot because I am not going to a bordello anytime soon; and

B) I am well.

22

TRICKLE-DOWN UPDATE

This morning, Momma discovered to her dismay that she was out of K-Cups for her coffeemaker. Thus, she decided she would have to venture out to get her required caffeine fix. She also decided that we would stop at the local pet salon on the way and get my nails clipped (compliments of Nanny). This went well, and the ladies even trimmed the matted fur by my ears. (Ahem!)

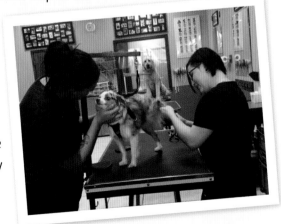

After my grooming visit, we were off to get coffee. That was not as easy as it might sound. We couldn't go to the nearest coffee shop because she was boycotting it. She felt she must make a statement due to the company's politically correct policies and practices with which she did not agree. Momma was really on her high horse about this. ("We're going to hit them where it hurts, Lina—in the pocketbook!")

She really needed a cup of coffee, though, and had already equivocated, deciding that buying just one cup from them wouldn't be a huge breach of her boycott—or make much of a difference to them. However, she really needed the K-Cups, too—and that was more of a major purchase—and a boost to the company bottom line. She decided to stick to her guns and go somewhere else.

Just then, though, Momma remembered that this PC company *did* give away a great doggie treat—and that the doggie treat was free! Now Momma was facing a really big dilemma—should she stand on principle or get a free treat for me (a dream come true for her)?

As we sped into their drive-through lane, I was already licking my chops.

Lina,
Lickin' Large

Yum!

23

ANOTHER HASTY EXIT

Momma was leaving town again, and she was bound and determined there would be no issues or drama this time for Dr. Becca or Nanny Becky. I don't think she was as concerned about inconveniencing them as she was about another humiliating blog post.

She almost made it. She had dog food, bones, and treats on hand. She even managed to leave a key for Dr. Becca so she could get in and out of the house to care for me. She was, however, running a tad behind as usual and was quite harried as she prepared to catch a ride to the airport.

Since I hadn't gone potty for an eternity, Momma decided she should take me out, even though she really couldn't spare the time. "Hurry *up*, Lina, let's go potty!" she commanded. She clipped me to my leash and then, forgetting what she was doing, ran to the kitchen to make coffee for the road. I trailed behind her, wondering what happened to my potty trip.

As Momma attempted to force the lid on the coffee cup, it squished out of her grasp, and the steaming-hot liquid flew everywhere. The counter, the cabinets, the drawers, the floor and her clothing were all drenched. The hot coffee even burned her skin in places, and for a brief moment, she thought of suing someone over this (the $3 million McDonald's case crossed her mind).

But first things first: in pain and nearly hysterical, Momma began hopping around and yelling, "Lina, Lina!" while I watched in horror (with my legs crossed). She became a maniac at this point, trying to rip her clothing off and clean up the mess at the same time. Taking me to the bathroom was the last thing on her mind.

When Momma finished wiping up the coffee and had care-fully selected a new traveling ensemble, she finally remembered that I was running around with my leash attached, desperately needing to go potty. Now *really* out of time, she pulled me out the door, shrieking, "Hurry, Lina, go potty quick—Momma's gotta leave right now!"

Luckily, I was able to perform, and off she went.

In her haste, Momma had left the coffee-soaked clothing, including her favorite sweater, in the laundry room. Suddenly, it occurred to her that if someone could take her sweater to the cleaners immediately (she had heard that time was of the essence with stains), they might be able to save it. Dr. Becca was coming over anyway, and Momma thought she would just call and give her a little heads-up. It seems Momma forgot that Dr. Becca has a full-time job and might not be up at 6:30 on a Saturday morning. Since Dr. Becca didn't answer, she left a message and then called Becky—just in case *she* was standing at the ready with nothing to do.

When Momma got to the airport and—temporarily—came to her senses, she realized that a stained sweater might not be the national emergency she thought it was, and she texted the Bs (Dr. Becca and Becky) to apologize and explain. (She was also a little nervous that this might be the last straw for both of

them.) By then, however, the Bs had come to the rescue, and the precious sweater was already at the cleaners.

The morning's emergency over, Momma's worries now turned to the blog. She texted Dr. Becca, warning her that I'd better not broadcast her latest fiasco and referring to me as "the Little Tattle*tail*."

Me with my new hedgehog!

With Momma finally out of my fur, things calmed down at home, and my week with the Bs progressed nicely. They often reported to Momma on our activities, in case her thoughts ever turned to me. Dr. Becca told Momma that she took me along to run errands and even to work ("To *what*?" Momma queried) one day. Dr. Becca also sent a

Me with my pink harness

photo of my new Halloween toy, and my new *size-appropriate* pink harness.

Don't tell Momma I said this, but I saw her studying the picture when trying to figure out how to put it on me.

Mercifully, there are never any emergencies when the Bs are in charge, and we had a fun, relaxing week. All too soon, though, Momma's (and my!) vacation was over, and she returned. In case you are wondering, the stain did not come out of the sweater, the replacement cost of which can only hurt the bottom Lina.

Lina, The Little Tattletail

WOOFDA!

A RUFF WEEK FOR MOMMA

You have to give her credit. Sometimes Momma tries to cut spending on herself (on select items), and sometimes she even tries to do good for others. Somehow, though, things always come back to bite her . . .

The Drug Dilemma

Recently, Momma switched insurance companies, and she thought this would be a perfect opportunity to cut costs. She had enrolled in, well, let's just call it the Big Government benefit (the kind she scoffed at when given to others) she had been waiting for her entire life. She was looking forward to what she thought would be free health care! She soon learned, however, that health care was not the bargain or as simple as she'd thought it would be.

When it came to selecting a cost plan to partner with Big Government's benefit, she was going to be selective. "No wasted premiums" was her motto. Therefore, when Big Insurance asked if she wanted an Rx plan on her policy, she said emphatically, "*No!*" She wasn't about to pay for a plan she would not use. In her mind, she is still in her twenties and doesn't use medication (none of those unsightly pill organizers with the giant letters for her!). Plus, Big Insurance was charging about $50 extra per month for the drug plan—money that could well be spent elsewhere—on clothing, for example (see next page).

Her new austerity plan worked for about a week. Then she discovered there was a prescription she needed after all. (I'm thinking—hoping—some sort of mood stabilizer.)

When she went to pick up the pills, Momma had a rude awakening. The pharmacist handed her a little white bag and announced, "That will be $416."

Gripping the counter, Momma croaked, "There must be some mistake" (the same reaction she has when her credit card is being declined). There was no mistake, however—she just didn't have drug coverage anymore. Who knew drugs were so expensive?

On the way home, Momma did the math in her head and decided maybe the Rx thing was the way to go after all. She was just praying that she wouldn't have to pay a penalty—a consequence she previously chose to ignore—for adding it after her initial enrollment. She also hoped it was still the open enrollment period. Why did this insurance stuff have to be so complicated? In the back of her mind, of course, she was already blaming Obamacare.

Resigning herself to the fact that she had made a mistake, Momma dialed Big Insurance back up. When she finally got through to a human being, she had to do the whole enrollment process again, which took the better part of the morning. After a few torturous moments on the phone with Momma—and wanting to end the call, I'm sure—the representative inquired of Momma, "Do you know how to use the Internet, dear?"

The fact that Big Insurance's representative was lumping Momma into a category of elderly people that may not even know how to use the Internet was almost more than she could bear. She didn't know whether to laugh or cry. She stuck with it, though, not wanting to hang up and have to start the hellish process all over again. (At this point, I rewarded her with a face lick!)

The Closet Catastrophe

The drug matter put to bed for the moment, Momma turned to another project she hated—cleaning out her closet.

She knew it was necessary, because her closet was jammed with stuff she never wore. She also rationalized that if she got rid of some old stuff, she would be justified in getting some new items—applying her own backward version of the rule mandating that if one bought something new, one must get rid of something old. And Momma had a plan for the disposal of the old clothing—she would give it to Goodwill ("It's time to give back, Lina").

Filled with warm feelings of, well, goodwill, Momma hurriedly pulled things off hangers, out of drawers, and off shelves, and stuffed them into shopping bags. She wanted to get this done and get it done fast—like ripping the Band-Aid off quickly!

The day after Momma's frenzied purging, she went to put on her favorite pair of jeans. The only problem was that they were no longer in her closet. Realizing instantly what had happened, she howled, "No, Lina, no!"

How could she get them back? Would Goodwill allow her to go through the bags she'd dropped off the day before? Would they even still be there? Would she have to buy back her own jeans if she found them?

Me shopping for a pill organizer and jeans

Getting no good answers over the phone, Momma showed up bright and early to shop for her jeans at Goodwill (*Really,* she thought, *could things get any worse?*). To no avail, as it turned out—Momma never got her jeans back (another face lick from me). Luckily, she has some space for new ones in her closet.

Lina, Momma's Rock

WOOFDA!

25

THE MYSTERY VISITOR

The other night as Momma and I watched Fox News, I noticed something outside our living room window. I sprang to my paws and glared mightily at the creature. My ears shot up, my fur stood on end, and my legs twitched. I looked at Momma expectantly. Even she could tell something was up, but she dismissed it, saying, "Oh, Lina, that's just your reflection in the glass you see," and went back to what was undoubtedly "fair and balanced" news.

Then I saw the same shadowy figure appear around the corner at another window. Instantly, I hopped off the couch for a better look—but what I saw was so scary that I immediately hightailed it (well, I ran fast) back to Momma, emitting a ferocious little growl.

My nightly in-dog-trination

Now I had her attention. Although annoyed that this incident was interrupting her right-wing program, she decided to investigate. Remembering that bad guys can see in when the lights are on, she snapped them off and turned the deck lights on. Not surprisingly, she saw nothing—I mean, who/what stands there bathed in bright light, waiting to be identified? Then Momma walked to the back door and turned on the security system. As she walked past the front door, she saw an animal approach and gaze in.

Yikes! she thought. *Is that the big gray cat that I've been seeing in the neighborhood for weeks? Probably not*, she reasoned—*too big. And too feral looking with a pointy nose and beady little eyes. What is it, then?* (Momma grew up on a farm but somehow managed to learn nothing about animals.)

As the animal continued to stare in through the door, Momma tried to identify it. (I had wisely stayed in the living room guarding us against a possible attack from the back of the house.) She thought that it could possibly be a wolf, raccoon, fox, coyote, cougar, lynx or dingo (just kidding—even Momma knew better!), but she really didn't know what any of them looked like.

As the animal sauntered away, Momma took one last look and tried to memorize the image, but it was hopeless. Five seconds later, she couldn't even remember if it had a tail. Then she had an inspiration—she would Google it! Truth be told, that search engine pretty much does all her thinking these days.

She plugged in "small wild mammals in Minnesota" and clicked on *Images* (she was pretty proud that she knew of this feature). At this point, Momma didn't even really care what the animal was anymore—she just wanted to appear knowledgeable to her friends—being a farm girl and all. Admitting that she didn't know if the thing was a wild animal or a big gray cat (which she hadn't yet ruled out) would just be too embarrassing.

Momma had heard that coyotes were appearing all over the Twin Cities. *Why wouldn't they be in our backyard?* she thought. She would go with that. It fit in nicely with her narrative—coyotes were known to go after small animals, so now she'd be fearlessly protecting me from a dangerous predator. Yup, it was a coyote!

Once Momma had finished watching the nightly lineup of Fox programs, she suddenly remembered me and had a frightening thought: she still had to take me out to go potty once more! Could she make me hold it all night? Force me to go on the pee pad in the laundry room? (Not that *she* was scared, but she had to protect me, after all.)

We did end up going outside for potty, but only just outside the door where it was well lit. When I wasn't able to go within about seven seconds, Momma pulled me back inside, explaining, "It's not that long 'til morning, Lina."

We haven't seen the animal since, but now Momma is talking about buying a gun, pointing out that she is going to exercise her Second Amendment rights. I just hope she can tell a Toy Aussie from a big gray cat.

Lina, Guard Dog

WOOFDA!

26

CHRISTMAS CONUNDRUMS

Momma is glad Christmas is over. Not that she doesn't celebrate the birth of the Christ Child and enjoy all the related festivities; she just finds that Christmastime gets more stressful and complicated every year.

First, there is the yearly debate about whether one can still say "Merry Christmas" or should play it safe with "Happy Holidays"—or something even more milquetoast like "Happy Winter Solstice." Actually, though, this is not a big dilemma for Momma, who freely (and pointedly) calls out, "Merry Christmas!" to everyone she sees. ("*We* are celebrating Christmas, Lina—others can say what they want.")

To Momma, worrying about what to say so as not to offend was a waste of time and detracted from the true meaning of

Christmas. She had other things on her mind—there was shopping to be done (some even for others), self-promoting Christmas cards to be ordered, and cocktail parties to attend.

Next, just like clockwork, the annual legal battles over religious displays in public places pop up. Just as predictably, the issue of school music programs arises every year—what type of music is permissible—indeed, is a program allowed at all? Surely someone would be left out even with the best intentions and efforts humanly possible. Momma fondly remembers the good old days when she taught music in North Dakota and could have the kids sing whatever she wanted—at their *Christmas* program. Come to think of it, she bets they can still do that in North Dakota! Maybe she would just move back there. (For once, I'm on board with Momma—I hear they have almost no lakes.)

While tiresome and annoying, these are not the biggest issues confronting Momma at Christmas. The one that takes the cake (speaking of food) is making dinner for her family on Christmas Eve.

It used to be so easy—she'd buy a honey-baked ham at a specialty store, some pre-made Swedish meatballs (Momma's family is Norwegian but she could never find/didn't know if there was such a thing as Norwegian meatballs—close enough, though, she thought), some pre-made mashed potatoes (always being careful to remove the store packaging and imply she made them herself), and call it a day.

When relatives asked what they could bring, she'd assign a time-consuming item like a complicated hors d'oeuvre, salad, or vegetable to round out the menu. For dessert, she'd usually take the chocolates out of a box she got from someone else and arrange them on a platter as though she had just thrown together some gourmet chocolate truffles. ("People don't really need dessert anyway, Lina.")

As with the rest of Christmas, though, dinner was more complicated now. Out of the nine family members she served on Christmas, at least four had special dietary needs. Two required food to be gluten-free. Those same two were also lactose intolerant. Two others were vegans, although one would occasionally make exceptions—like when someone brought something especially tasty that was not allowed on his or her diet. Plus two were organic farmers, which also had to be factored into the mix. And one ate only dog food.

First off, Momma had only a vague idea what these terms entailed. *Gluten-free*, she was pretty sure, meant no wheat, but were other grains allowed? *Lactose intolerant* meant no dairy, she thought, but really what constituted *dairy*? And *vegan* totally threw her—she knew there was almost nothing they *could* eat (really, how did they stay alive?)—but she was reasonably sure veggies were okay—but only if they were organic, right? And did anyone require that their food be pasture-raised? When Momma first heard that term being used by two granola crunchers at the grocery store, she was sure they were confused and corrected them, saying "It's pronounced *pasteurized*." I'm glad I was at home.

Luckily (as is usually the case with Momma), others came to the rescue for Christmas Eve dinner this year, bringing enough food items that were lacking in one or more prohibited ingredient that everyone was able to eat. For her part, Momma's big concession was that she made her own mashed potatoes and, being careful to stick to prescribed dietary guidelines, did not use butter or cream. (She was in something of a snit later, though, after being told that butter is okay for the lactose intolerant—but come to think of it, that wouldn't have worked for the vegan crowd, would it?) Anyway, she found a recipe online for "Delicious Creamy Dairy-Free Mashed Potatoes" and dutifully whipped them up. The fraudulently named and nearly inedible recipe basically called for potatoes and chicken stock. But whatever. And the vegans did not need to know about the chicken stock.

Pawning off the meatballs on me

Unlike Momma, I am sensitive to the religion of others—Hanaramakwanzmas and Happy 2016!

Lina

WOOFDA!

27

I'M ALL EARS

When I was only a few weeks old, Momma's "friend" Jane took one look at me and said, "Do you think she'll ever grow into her ears?" When Momma got over her irritation, she took a closer look and realized they really *were* quite large. As time went on, and I didn't grow into them, Momma nicknamed me "Little Big Ears."

My ears fully un*furl*ed!

When I started my blog, they became a really big deal for Momma—she had pie-in-the-sky ideas of making money off the big-ear concept. Therefore, you can imagine that what happened a few days ago was a near tragedy in her mind.

We had just returned to Florida when Momma decided to buy something for me (probably to keep up with the other doggie mommas in her building). She swung into the local pet store and found a cute T-shirt (which would be great if I *wanted* to wear a tee) with MARCO ISLAND emblazoned on it. Not knowing if it would fit—and not wanting to have to return it, Momma insisted that the saleslady try the tee on another dog who weighed about the same as I do. It fit perfectly, and Momma shelled out the money.

Arriving home, Momma called out, "Lina, wait 'til you see what I bought you!" and she pulled my new tee from the bag. (It should have been a clue to her that this was a bad idea when my ears fell and I ran into the next room to hide.) Undeterred, Momma found me and tugged the shirt over my head and tucked my little legs into the openings. Satisfied that it fit—and picturing showing me off to her friends—she exclaimed, "Don't you look *fetching*, Lina?" and went about her putzing.

Meanwhile, I noticed that something was wrong—my left ear felt funny—so I started whipping my head back and forth to get rid of the sensation. After about five minutes of this, Momma looked at me and said, "Okay, Lina, let's take it off for now." She removed the dreaded tee, but the strange feeling in my ear did not go away, and I continued to vigorously shake my head.

Now I really had Momma's attention. "What's wrong, Lina?" she asked, taking a good look at me. At this point, she saw that my left ear no longer stood up like the right. In fact, it was plastered against my head! Momma went into a panic and wailed, "Oh, my God, Lina, what's wrong with your ear?" Momma was terrified that her pulling the tee over my head had done some permanent damage and, frankly, was extremely concerned that our "Little Big Ears" franchise was in danger.

Seeing no alternative, Momma called the emergency animal hospital, who predictably recommended that she bring me in. So off we went, with me in the front seat so Momma could keep an eye on the precious ear and see if it popped up again.

When we arrived, Momma carried me up to the front desk of the hospital. The two receptionists looked at us quizzically and asked what the problem was. When Momma explained that there was something wrong with one of my ears, they paged a nurse who came into the waiting room to take a look.

Admittedly, it didn't look like much was wrong, so the nurse asked Momma to tell him what was going on. "Well, I bought a new T-shirt for Lina and tried it on her, and now one of her ears won't stand up anymore," Momma explained and added helpfully, "and she keeps shaking her head to straighten it out again."

As you can imagine, every eye in the place was now on us, all ears perked up (except for mine). The nurse looked at us as if we had just dropped in from Mars. Also, I'm pretty sure I heard a few snickers from the other dog owners. Seriously, who brings their dog in because one of her ears won't stand up?

Also, by now my errant ear was looking better—it was at least at half-mast. Just so the nurse didn't think Momma was totally crazy, I shook my head emphatically to demonstrate that something wasn't right. Although he had pretty much determined there was nothing wrong with me—indeed that maybe he should call security—the nurse invited us to have a seat and wait for the doctor, warning us that it would be about an hour (it was three).

At the point, Momma was wavering. It didn't appear the nurse was concerned—and did she really want to spend Saturday evening at the animal hospital? That all changed, however, when she learned that the young, hot Dr. Garny who had seen us before was on duty. (Am I the only one who suspects that she knew this all along?) Suddenly, a three-hour wait on a Saturday night for a likely unnecessary $150 exam seemed like a gift from God.

When Dr. Garny finally appeared, Momma repeated the ridiculous *tail* about the tee and the lopsided ears. He listened patiently, if warily, but as expected couldn't find much wrong—even though I did the head-shake for him, too. Nevertheless, he gave me an anti-inflammatory shot before sending us on our way. To Momma's disappointment, he did not say we needed a follow-up exam.

Lina, The Author Formerly Known as "Little Big Ears"

WOOFDA!

ANOTHER MEDICAL "EMERGENCY"

few days after our misguided trip to the vet for my flattened ear, we had another mishap. This time, Momma was absentmindedly throwing the ball for me to fetch when it glanced off the wall and struck me in the eye. Although it wasn't a hard hit, it hurt like heck, and I could only open the eye partway. Momma didn't like the look of it, but she decided not to rush me to the vet. (The fact that we would not be going to the weekend emergency hospital where Dr. Garny works also may have factored into her decision, but I'm not going to point any paws.)

Anyway, Momma was in no mood to be ridiculed—and to spend $150 if it wasn't absolutely necessary. "Just lie down and close your eyes for a while, Lina," she encouraged. I did, and amazingly my eye seemed better when I woke up—at least I could hold it open! Momma was thrilled—she was actually a little scared that another injury to me within a couple of weeks might raise a red flag with some watchdog group (pun intended).

By the next morning, however, my eye seemed worse—squinty and pink, and Momma rushed me to our regular doggie clinic. Luckily, there was no scratch so the vet just prescribed some eye drops and sent us home—$110 poorer.

I may have mentioned that my BFF in Florida is Gracie. She lives in our building, and I adore her. As we were driving home from the vet after the eye injury, Gracie's momma, Anne, called and asked if we could play. I looked at Momma beseechingly (with one eye), so she called the vet, who gave us permission, but with the caveat, "But keep the roughhousing to a minimum!"

Right, like that was going to happen. Here is an example of Gracie and me playing, but not *ruff*housing:

Anyway, we had the ill-advised playdate, and as expected, my eye was re-injured, requiring Momma to bring me in again. (Now she really *was* getting nervous about the authorities. She also noticed that the staff at the vet's office was not as friendly to her as on previous visits.) Although there was still no scratch in my eye, we left the clinic with specific instructions—no play-dates for four or five days! Momma was sure she was on some kind of watch list now. She was also out an additional $65.

By day four, Momma was getting tired of having me under-foot all the time, so she told Anne that I was good to go. We met her and Gracie out on the lawn for our long-awaited playdate. After a few minutes, Momma went inside to get her cell phone (and ostensibly some doggie toys) and left Anne to watch both of us. While she was gone, the twig I was chewing on got lodged crossways in the back of my mouth, causing me to gag and flail about. Anne was frantic—I was clearly in distress. When Momma saw me, she ran back inside to get the car keys.

By the time we got loaded, I had somehow expelled the stick, but now things were in motion, and they decided it was still a good idea to get me checked over. Momma begged Anne to go along for support (and so Momma could identify her as the caretaker when this latest injury occurred), so she and Gracie rode shotgun.

Upon our arrival, the tech whisked me into an exam room (and pointedly told Momma to stay in the waiting room). When I was gone, she hiss-whispered to Anne, "They'd better not charge me for *this* visit—the stick was gone, after all, and I've already spent a fortune here!"

After a few short minutes, the vet (this was the seasoned, handsome vet she'd tried to impress on our first visit to the clinic last year), brought me back out to the waiting room. After carefully scrutinizing Momma (*four* injuries in less than a month?), he informed her that there were scratches in my mouth but no stick, and I was fine.

Momma, sensing that she was being eyed with suspicion, immediately pointed to Anne and said that *she* had been supervising a playdate when I choked. Anne (always the grown-up of the two), graciously and unnecessarily shouldered the blame and apologized that I was hurt on her watch. At that point, the vet must have decided that I didn't have to be taken into protective custody, because he let me go home with Momma, but not without paying. Ouch!

The next day, Anne (she was pretty much co-parenting me by this time) suggested that Gracie and I have an indoor playdate—where I would be safer. Momma thought this was a great idea and told her to bring Gracie up to our place—after ten playdates at Anne's, she figured it might be her turn. Gracie and I had another rol*licking* good time, but I once again had a little too much fun, and now my other eye was hurt and half-shut. When Momma saw it, she practically cried—there was *no way* she was taking me to the vet again. She would be locked up. Instead, relying on a lick (mine) and a prayer (hers), she put some of those drops in my eye, and it healed!

Lina, Down (Dog) but Not Out!

WOOFDA!

29

HAPPY VALENTINE'S DAY, PLAYDATES, AND STROLLERS

Happy Valentine's Day from sunny Florida! Momma and I are now about halfway through our winter stay, and things have settled down nicely—one might woof miraculously. I have not been to see the vet in about two weeks (*see* "Another Medical 'Emergency,'" chapter 28), and Momma has stopped worrying about the authorities closing in on her, although one of her "friends"—CoCoa's momma, to be specific—threatened to turn her in to the ASPCA. (Momma chose to ignore her, though—saying she was just some liberal activist.)

Will you be my Valentine?

Gracie and Me

My time with Gracie is going spectacularly well. We play all the time—in fact, I basically live with Gracie and her family now. Even though Momma has good intentions about having Gracie over to play, I'd say the hound-hosting tally is about fifty to one in Anne's favor.

In Momma's defense, though, I don't think Anne quite trusts Momma to care for two dogs on her own. (And who can blame her? See the aforementioned chapter 28—in fact, see all previous chapters.) The first time she left Gracie with us, Anne hesitated at the door and nervously asked, "Are you sure I can leave Gracie? Will you be okay?" Momma said, "Sure," and then let us run wild and returned to online shopping—I'm not going to say for what or whom. Here I am getting the upper paw with Gracie for my beloved Lamb Chop:

Don't tell Anne, but after a few minutes of our raucous play, Momma was seriously considering drugging us with a few of the "calming aid" treats she has on hand.

(When) Will I Become a Stroller Dog?

The other day, Momma wanted to go to an art/craft show in Fort Myers and as a special treat decided to take me along. This was our first outing of this sort, but how hard could it be? She would just put me in my harness and have me heel smartly at her side, maybe visiting with a few dogs as we went. Plus, she had her cousin Janet along to help (actually, this was key and I'm sure influenced her decision—I'm just woofing).

Things didn't go exactly according to plan, however. I was quickly overwhelmed by the noise, the smells, the foot (and paw) traffic, and the hot weather. Pretty soon, I was panting and dragging, so Momma decided she'd better carry me. That lasted only until we reached the nearest wine stand, at which point she handed me off to Janet. After that, they continued to pass me back and forth, but I was getting heavy—I was *way* past being the tiny accessory dog Momma had dreamed of when she purchased me.

By now, Momma was frazzled and started eyeing women pushing dog strollers with envy. (She had always viewed these people as crazy and often proclaimed, "I'm never going to be *that* person Lina.") Today, however, Momma was reconsidering. It seemed every second doggie momma was pushing Fido along in a comfortable pram with a mesh top for good air flow and a great view. More importantly, the owners were free to visit, eat, drink, and browse the show unencumbered.

Finally, Momma couldn't take it any longer and started asking people if she could buy their strollers. When that failed (and people began to avoid her), Momma began looking around for a doggie stroller kiosk—*why* had no one ever thought of selling those at one of these stupid shows?

Luckily for all of us, we got rained out and had to leave early. Unluckily for me, I may be the pet of a crazy person, after all. I just hope there's room for Gracie!

Lina, Awaiting My New Ride

WOOFDA!

30

BILLGATE

The other day, fur was flying at our house. It seems Momma had let some bills lapse ("I didn't know they were due, Lina"), and now she had to face the music. She blamed her inattention on the fact that we were in Florida for the winter— apparently, she thought the bills do not accrue when one leaves the state (kind of like when an ostrich puts his head in the sand and thinks you can't see him).

Anyway, when Momma finally thought to have her mail forwarded to her, she saw in her mountain of paperwork that she had two statements from most of her creditors. She also observed that the latter of the two statements included penalties and interest. Momma, as usual and despite the serious nature of the notices, got on her high horse and declared, "They are barking up the wrong tree if they think I'm paying any late fees, Lina!" Nevertheless, even *she* knew that she had better get busy.

Momma grabbed her cell phone (luckily, she still had service) and started punching in numbers. I had an inkling that this was not going to go well and swiftly retreated to my crate.

Momma began with her cell phone provider. Sweating—she had noticed that the latest statement instructed her to PAY IMMEDIATELY!—she dialed customer service. She soon learned, though, that she would not be talking to a person but with a robot who informed her that she could speak in complete sentences (excuse me, but how would *he/it* know?). Momma got nowhere fast. No matter how many times she screamed, "Representative!" or stabbed the number 0 on her phone, she was not connected to a human being.

Finally, falling in line, she did her best to answer the robot's questions so she could be routed to a representative "trained to deal with her particular issue." When she finally got to tell the robot that she was calling to pay her bill, she was informed that she would be sent a text with a new temporary PIN code, and then she would have to create a new personalized passcode. (Momma was forced to do this twice, having gotten it wrong the first time around.) She was also informed that she would have to key in the last four digits of her Social Security number. Momma was almost apoplectic now, but she needed to keep her cool, and she soon realized that yelling (especially at a robot) did not help.

Finally, miraculously, Momma was connected to a person. Having gotten this far—and having had quite a bit of time to review her bill while she was on hold (and having been denied a waiver of her late fee), Momma decided that she had a few bones to pick with the highly trained bill payment specialist. For example, why was she being charged $10 for a phone number related to her iPad? After the specialist explained the fee and Momma still didn't have a clue what it was for, she surrendered, whimpering, "Please just tell me how much I owe so I can get off the phone."

When the specialist asked Momma how she wanted to pay, Momma, still smarting over the late fee and the other indignities of the phone call, curtly informed her that she would be paying with a credit card. This would mercifully have brought the matter to a close except for one tiny little detail: the card was denied. (At that point, Momma remembered that she also had two statements from said credit card company in the stack.) The by-now wary specialist then asked Momma if she had a different method of payment that she would like to use. Momma, struggling now to retain some measure of dignity, replied loftily that she would be using another major credit card. Then she held her breath until the charge was approved—she really couldn't remember where she stood with that card either.

A little panicked now, Momma quickly dialed up the company that had declined her card. To her amazement, she actually was able to speak to a person right away and explain herself ("I'm in Florida, so I didn't know I was behind on my payments"). Apparently, no excuse was too stupid for them, because not only did she get the late fee waived, she was also told she could start charging again the next day. Things were looking up!

The rest of the calls also went relatively smoothly: the electricity would not be turned off, and her homeowner's insurance would be reinstated. Another crisis/scandal in our lives had been averted. And not one person—or robot—had even mentioned bad credit or collection agency!

After the dust had settled, Momma spotted me observing the action from my crate. Immediately concerned about the blog, she asked enticingly, "Lina, would you like a treat?" Sadly, as a professional journalist, I was forced to turn her bribe down and tell my story.

Lina, Reporter

WOOFDA!

31

PRE-TRIP TROUBLE

After we got home from Florida in early April, I noticed that Momma was in more of a frenzy than usual. It didn't take me long to figure out that she was going on another trip.

First, she dialed up a bunch of salons to make maintenance appointments—you know the kind: hair, nails, skin, etc. Then I observed her studying a little black binder for instructions on how and what to pack for a twenty-four-day trip. I next saw that she was spending an inordinate amount of time in her closet (and that's *saying* something) looking through clothes, shoes, handbags and totes. The dead giveaway, of course, was when she brought out the suitcases.

Since Momma had failed to share the news of her trip ("I didn't want you to feel bad, Lina"), I couldn't help but wonder what type of arrangements she had made for me. When she saw the look of concern on my face, she reassured me that there was nothing to worry about. "Yes, Lina, Momma's going on a little trip, but she won't be gone long. And guess what? Dr. Becca will be staying with you, and Nanny Becky will also be around." (I know that she had heard that dogs have no concept of time, but even I could tell that twenty-four days was a tad long.)

Unfortunately, a couple of days before she was to leave, Momma was forced to turn her attention away from her non-stop prepping to me. Out of the blue, I began having episodes during which I had trouble getting my breath. At first, Momma thought the problem would just go away or was something I would have to live with based on comments of several dog owners that it was likely just a "reverse sneeze." Huh?

Momma wasn't satisfied with that explanation either and decided to take me to the local vet for a look. He couldn't find anything wrong but thought the problem might be allergies and suggested that we try Children's Benadryl. Momma, however, drawing on her vast amount of medical knowledge, decided the problem was not allergies and declined to buy the drug.

The day before she was to leave, I was having the breathing problems more frequently, and Momma, half-crazy by now because her big trip was looming large, concluded that she'd better bite the bullet and take me to a specialist. I'm not sure how, but she roped Becky into going along.

We had booked an appointment at the nearest specialty clinic, which turned out to be in Eden Prairie, a suburb southwest of Minneapolis and not too far from our house. The internist there said they'd probably have to do a rhinoscopy to determine what was wrong (I never experienced the breathing problems while with the vets, so they didn't have much to go on). The internist further explained that I would have to be anesthetized for the test, which would consist of putting a speculum in my nostrils to view the inside of my nose!

By now, we were *both* sick—me at the thought of the scope going into my head and Momma because of the inevitable astronomical bill. Nevertheless, she did have that trip coming up the next day so she had little choice but to approve the horrific test.

We were all set to go forward when the clinic informed us that their rhinoscopy equipment was on the blink. If we wanted to proceed, we would have to go to their sister clinic in Blaine, a northern suburb about forty-five minutes away. As far as Momma was concerned, it might as well have been in another country. (Even though Momma is from a tiny town about five hours north of Minneapolis, she thought of Blaine as in "the boonies" and dreaded the thought of going to an animal clinic there.)

Out of options by now, though, we piled into the car and headed to Blaine. Momma casually looked at the little map she had been given from the first clinic and announced to Becky that she knew the way. Well, it turns out that she didn't, and she took the wrong exit as we were approaching Minneapolis. Pretty soon, instead of speeding up to Blaine on I-94, we were driving past all the bars, strip clubs and theaters downtown on Hennepin Avenue. *Really?* I thought, *Would it have been so hard to just plug the address into the GPS?* I'm sure Becky, who was not at all happy with this turn of events, was thinking the same thing. (She did have a family and her own schedule, after all.)

After driving around downtown Minneapolis for about an hour in the middle of a busy workday, we somehow ended up on the freeway again and headed north. When we finally, mercifully, arrived at the clinic in Blaine, Momma quickly came off her high horse. She could tell that this was a top-notch facility with a great staff. And we loved our vet (even though she *did* knock me out for the dastardly set of tests I was about to endure).

Here we are before.

And me trying to get my paws under me again afterward.

In addition to the rhinoscopy, they also conducted a series of X-rays, a CT scan and a nasal biopsy, after which they informed Momma that my nasal passages were somewhat pink and inflamed. Despite this finding, however, the internist was not sure of the cause. She did suspect allergies, though, and therefore suggested we pick up some—you guessed it—Children's Benadryl!

Momma, by now staring at a bill for $2,200, was beside herself. "Becky," she wailed, "if only I had given her the Benadryl before, think of the money I could have saved!" (And *I* was thinking, *If only you hadn't booked a twenty-four-day trip, think of the money you could have saved.*) Anyway, after she reluctantly paid the bill, we rushed out to the car, all of us anxious to get home.

Our excitement for the day wasn't quite over yet, however. Momma understandably was by now pretty upset over the day's events. I was sick, she was out at least $2,200, she had probably used up all the goodwill Becky had left in her, it was 8:00 p.m., and (this was the clincher) she had not yet finished shopping or packing for her trip the next day. So what happened next really shouldn't have been a surprise.

When we finally pulled into the garage that evening, Momma could not find her keys. In fact, they were not in the car with us. "That can't be, Becky," she croaked. After all, we had just driven home in the car (which had a keyless starter). "The car wouldn't drive without the keys, would it?"

Well, it turned out, it would. God only knows how it happened, but Momma must have started the car, put the keys on the roof or hood or trunk or on the street, and driven off. Luckily, Becky had keys for our house and was able to get us in and on her way. Now Momma had a new worry, however—the cost of a new key fob, plus the fact that her keys for everything were somewhere in Blaine, possibly in someone else's possession!

Unbelievably, though, Becky (who as usual mopped up Momma's messes for her) got the keys back. She had called the vet's office the next day, and after explaining the situation, an employee found our keys in their parking lot. (Am I the only one thinking they are probably still talking about us?)

In the end, I must report that the Benadryl did not clear up the inflammation—and Momma was happy to be vindicated. It turned out I had an infection, and with the help of the vet, Dr. Becca, and Becky, I switched medicine and had a complete recovery!

When the dust finally settled, as it always does when Momma leaves town, I was able to enjoy my time with the Bs as I always do.

Lina, Survivor

WOOFDA!

32

NEW FURRY FRIENDS

Even though (or maybe because?) Momma was gone for a good chunk of the spring on her circle-the-globe trip, I have been having a great time. Besides getting to spend time with my favorites, Dr. Becca and Nanny Becky, I made three new furry friends!

The Foster Dog

I actually met the first one right before Momma left on her trip. She had been carefully planning her upcoming golf schedule upon her return and was scouting out various doggie day care facilities in which to place (dump) me. She finally found one nearby that she thought was acceptable because it had a separate play area for small dogs. Excited, she called to enroll me.

Momma's excitement turned to exasperation, however, when she was told that she first must bring me in for an interview. She had a change of heart, though, when she found out that if I passed my interview, Momma would be required to leave me (on a complimentary basis!) at the day care for at least three hours to see how I got along with others. She quickly decided that screening was a good practice, after all.

Unfortunately, we did have a little stumbling block before my stay when Momma insisted on touring the day care facility. When we got to the play area, she noticed that one of the dogs was quite large. Why was he not in the big dog area? Momma wanted to know. In response to her pointed questioning, the manager, who had been enlisted to help with the tour (no surprise there), explained that the dog was a foster dog and was too nervous to be with the big dogs. Despite Momma's misgivings about me being in an area with a big, nervous dog, she suddenly remembered that I could stay there for three hours—free—so she'd better take advantage of it and leave! I'd have to learn to take care of myself sooner or later, right?

When Momma came to get me five hours later, the staff said I did well and handed her my report card. The report stated that I am a social butterfly and that my best friend was—you guessed it—the big foster dog!

Winnie

Shortly after Momma left, I had another nice surprise: Dr. Becca adopted a rescue dog! She is a little wiener dog named Edwina, which Dr. Becca had shortened to Winnie—ignoring Momma's near insistence that the dog be called Eddie.

Winnie is about my size and age, and we had a great time together. I was tickled to have company and helped show Winnie the ropes as she got used to her new life with Dr. Becca. Here are some shots of us getting to know one another!

Annie

Next I met Annie, a puppy who was recently adopted by Momma's friends Erik and Cheryl. She is a lab and sheltie mix and is also a rescue dog. She is just a little bigger than I am, and we have quite the time chasing each other around the yard! She is a sweetheart.

I got to know Annie when Becky took me on a walk with her and Cheryl and again when she came over for a playdate. Erik also brought over a new paddleboard, and Momma had grandiose plans for us all to go out on the water together—never mind that Annie had never even seen a lake before and the fact that I'm not a huge fan.

Luckily, it was too windy, so we went out on the pontoon instead. That would have been fun had I not been all decked out in my pointless protective gear. Really, what were the chances I'd end up in the water? On the other paw, Annie was able to stay cool—and *see*—so she got to enjoy her first boat ride.

I am so looking forward to summer and more playdates. I know this is very cliché, but all of a sudden, I have more friends than I can shake a stick at.

Lina, Social Butterfly

WOOFDA!

33

ANOTHER VET VISIT AND THE PET CAM

Tummy Trouble

L ast Saturday did not go well. First, I threw up in bed. Momma, who wanted to avoid washing the bedclothes, quickly cupped her hands under my mouth to catch the vomit. Naturally, it didn't work, and the vomit ended up on the bed *and* the carpet when it dripped through her fingers on the way to the bathroom. (Nanny Becky suggested that maybe in the future Momma should keep a towel on the bed—just a thought, she said.)

An hour later, I threw up again. Momma still didn't think too much about it, assuming that I had eaten something that didn't agree with me the day before. Therefore, she went ahead and fed me, but I promptly threw up again—this time in my little doggie bed (which she also had to wash). When Momma saw the mess, it finally sank in that I might actually be sick. Her next thought was, *Oh, God, it's Saturday, and that means if I bring her to the emergency hospital, it will cost a fortune!*

She was not about to make that trip if she didn't have to and decided to wait and see what happened. What happened wasn't good—I puked all over her overpriced area rug in the living room. When Momma found me there surrounded by little puddles of green-and-brown slime, she shrieked, "Lina, no!" She was so upset that her precious rug (I wonder how *it* fit into her budget) might be ruined that she totally forgot I was sick or frankly that she even had a dog.

Realizing that things were—once again—exceeding her ability to cope, she called Becky, who as usual dropped everything and came over. After comforting me, cleaning up the mess, and locating a nearby animal hospital, Becky loaded me in the car, and off we went. On the way over, Momma threatened to sell me for about the one hundredth time. Becky, having heard it all before, told me not to worry and gave me a big hug.

Another one of Momma's friends, Cheryl (Annie's momma), who had told us about the hospital, was waiting there to see how things were going and had been inside to ask if we were there yet. Seriously, I wonder what the staff must think. How helpless must a person be to have someone *waiting* for them at the hospital and a nanny along to help care for a dog with an upset stomach?

Nevertheless, things turned out okay, and $217 later, I was on the road to recovery. Don't be surprised, though, if you see me on eBay.

The Pet Cam

The other day, Momma had the bright idea to put a camera in our house so she could observe my activities while she was away. She did a little quick research, ordered the camera, and downloaded the accompanying app for her phone. This made her feel good, by the way—very tech savvy—almost like she could be a member of the Geek Squad.

When the camera arrived and Momma finally figured out how to use it, it dawned on her that she could not only keep an eye on me but on the house as well! Thus, she had cheaply—and accidentally—installed a surveillance system and could now see if an intruder had broken in (in case the intruder happened to be glued to the spot in the corner by my bed).

Momma was especially excited that the little camera included a speaker and laser light. The laser was supposed to be a little "toy" that would enable owners to play with their pets remotely. And with the speaker, she could talk to me while she was away (although I don't know how I was supposed to hear her over the Rush Limbaugh program that was always blaring in my ears).

Momma was really digging her new gadget at this point and tested out it out by repeatedly yelling, "Lina!" into her phone. After a little delay, the speaker also yelled out, "Lina!" This confused me, to say the least, because now her voice was coming at me from all directions and I didn't know where to look or what she wanted.

Momma was pleased with the device, though, and thought that just maybe—in a pinch—it could take the place of expensive doggie day care! She could have me chase the little red dot around the room for exercise (never mind that I'm not a cat), and could talk to me as though she were still at home ("Take a nap, Lina," and "Don't go potty in the house, Lina").

Momma couldn't wait to try out her new built-in dog sitter/surveillance system when she arrived at the golf course the next day. At least every other hole, she would activate the camera app and insist that her friends look at me. I was just a little dot on the screen, by the way—Momma didn't have an extension cord that would allow her to move the camera closer to my bed—where I constantly slept while she was gone. At least I *used* to constantly sleep. Now I am awakened every few minutes when Momma's disembodied voice screeches, "Hi, Lina!" causing me to whip my head around and look for her. Is it any wonder that I get an upset stomach?

I wonder how long it will take her to realize that nothing much goes on during her frequent absences and she gets tired of the gadget. I also wonder how long it will be before no one will play golf with her anymore. I'm just woofing.

Lina, Longing for Peace and Quiet . . .

WOOFDA!

34

MOMMA'S STRUGGLE TO STAY RELEVANT

I've been with Momma for nearly two—how shall I woof it?— incredible years now. For the most part, she's managed to stay on top of things, but lately she has been in a funk about life in the twenty-first century. It's just too complicated, she has concluded—too much work to try and keep up. "It's almost like having a full-time job, Lina," she whimpers. Which of course "begs" the question—how would she know?

Momma is especially upset about the lightning-fast changes in communication and technology ("Things used to be so simple, Lina—a television with three channels and a rotary dial desk phone—did we really need more?"). But now every aspect of her life, it seems, leaves her in a constant state of bewilderment and frustration. She laments that even her car is way over her head. She can barely get the radio (if that's what it's still called) or the air conditioning turned on. And does she really have time to be pulling over every few feet to read the operator's manual?

Another of Momma's pet peeves these days is the onslaught of social media. "I don't like the way it's intruding on our lives, Lina," she complains. The reason she is so resentful, of course, is that she doesn't understand it.

For example, the other day, we were filling up on gasoline, and she saw that the ad by the gas pump encouraged her to "Follow us on Facebook." *What?* she thought. *Even if I knew how, why would I go home and get on my computer to find out what's new at Super America on Facebook? Don't I have enough to do already?* she inwardly seethed.

Similarly, she recently heard the host of a news broadcast direct viewers to "like us" on Facebook. *Really, I can't just watch the news anymore and be done with it?* she fumed. *Do people really drop everything they are doing and get on one of their devices to "vote" for the stupid program (especially one that is not Fox News)?*

Momma becomes even more exasperated when she opens an email from a merchant or a webpage and sees all the tiny social media symbols at the bottom of the page urging her to "stay connected" via Facebook, Twitter, Pinterest, Instagram, Google, Google+, Google Play ("Just how many Google things can there be, Lina?"), Tumblr and YouTube. Should she choose one? Two? All of them? Will she lose touch with the world if she opts not to? What are they, anyway?

Another thing that sends her into orbit is all the choices one must make just by carrying out a purchase. Which credit card should she use? (Note to Momma—the one that is not maxed out.) Does she hand it to the sales associate or use the little machine? Does she slide or insert it? Invariably, she does the wrong thing and the condescending associate—who addresses her as *dear*—must correct her. And could she just once remove her inserted card from the machine before it honks at her, notifying everyone in line that she doesn't know what she's doing?

Then there's the receipt dilemma. Does she want it by paper? Email? Both? This drives her crazy. If she takes it in paper format, the young, hip salesperson will think she is a doddering old fool or a Republican who doesn't care about the environment. (Editor's note: "If the shoe fits, Momma, wear it.") If she chooses email, will she be able to find it in the stack of 2,132 unopened items currently sitting on her iMac, when she makes the (inevitable) return? And she'll have to print it then, anyway, won't she? And hasn't she made enough decisions just by picking which pair of shoes to buy?

"It's enough to make me want to stay home and crawl under a rock, Lina." But not enough to make her want to quit shopping, I'm sure.

Lina, Trying to Keep Momma In Line and Online

WOOFDA!

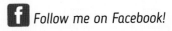 *Follow me on Facebook!*

35
TURNING TWO!

Last year, Momma threw an attention-grabbing party for my first birthday (complete with handouts of my new business cards) in high hopes of upping my blog readership and snagging advertisers. Like most of Momma's little schemes, however, it didn't work, and she put her blog push on the back burner.

Consequently, my birthday this year was not a big deal to her. In fact, she almost forgot about it altogether. She only remembered when her friend—and my legal counsel—Uncle Chuck, handed her a gift bag for me. Momma, momentarily caught off guard, quickly recovered and said coolly, "Oh, yes, of course, Lina's second birthday is coming up—I'll give this to her." Awkward.

Momma was also reminded of my birthday when Nanny Becky showed up with a snazzy new collar and handcrafted scarf! Here I am with my Jimmy Chew from Chuck's dog, Willie, and modeling my hound couture from Becky's family.

Well, this got Momma thinking—two priceless gifts . . . how could she top that? Then she had a brainstorm. She would give me the gift of time with her. The next day, she announced to me, "Lina, I am going to stay home with you *all* day on your birthday. And we'll even go to Chuck & Don's and pick out a nice present." (Now that I think about it, I'm surprised she hasn't embarrassed me by hitting them up for advertising.)

The day at home with Momma didn't exactly end up being the quality time I had envisioned. In fact, she had decided that as long as she was going to be stuck at home with me all day, she would go a little Martha Stewart and can some salsa. (A friend had given her a bunch of tomatoes and peppers, and she would take advantage of the free food.)

It may go without woofing, but the canning did not go exactly according to plan. (My first clue that trouble might be a-paw was when I saw her Google "how to can salsa.") It was no surprise, then, that there were a few mishaps along the way, including the broken jar in the water bath incident. At least neither of us was injured. Unfortunately, though, the finished product looked more like tomato broth than salsa. How any-one could scoop it up with a chip was beyond me. That didn't faze, Momma, however—she would pass it off to relatives as Christmas presents.

When Momma finally finished making salsa, she took me to Chuck & Don's to find a gift. I know it sounds a tad ungrateful to say that she grabbed the first thing she saw, but it wouldn't be far from the truth. It seems the salsa production had taken about four hours longer than it should have and cut into my shopping time. Anyway, here's my new ball.

On a brighter note, Nanny also remembered my birthday with a doggie e-card. I'm really diggin' it, as you can tell. To view the action, just go online and click on

https://linasdogblog.com/2016/09/04/turning-two/

Thanks to everyone who made my birthday special!

Lina, Ready to Embark on Another Exciting Year with Momma

WOOFDA!

36

MOMMA AND THE RYDER CUP

The Prelude

A few months ago, Momma signed up to work as a marshal at the Ryder Cup. It would feature the best European and American golfers in the world. Visions of Phil, Ricky, Jordan, and Bubba danced in her head. Momma would go to any length to see the action up close and personal—even if it meant working as a marshal—something she knew she was not cut out for.

Thinking big, Momma signed up to work Thursday, Friday, Saturday and Sunday. As excited as she was, though, Momma was equally nervous. What if she made a huge mistake and disgraced her country? Oh, well, she would worry about that when the time came.

As the event drew near, Momma got so caught up in Cup spirit that she temporarily forgot her reservations. She was especially thrilled when she learned that she would be required to buy a new Ralph Lauren golf shirt and jacket. Perfect! ("I know I'm on a budget, Lina, but I can't help it if I'm *forced* to buy a new outfit, can I?")

When Momma finally buckled down and read the Ryder Cup materials, she realized that she was right to be concerned— the marshal job had a lot of responsibilities. In fact, there were two training sessions—one at Chaska High School and one on-site at Hazeltine.

The training at CHS was first. Momma picked up her smart new uniform and headed proudly to the auditorium for the presentation. The speakers told the participants that the marshals had an important job to do and gave them an overview of their duties. Although she struggled mightily to concentrate, Momma's mind kept wandering (would she look okay in the new Polo outfit?) and about the only thing that registered was the volunteer's motto—"Greet, assist, and thank." "That's the main thing, anyway, Lina," she rationalized to me later that night (with just a hint of worry in her voice).

A few weeks later, Momma headed out to the on-site training. Even though she had been out to Hazeltine before, she was worried she might get lost. She was to look for parking lot A-3, she thought. Or was it C-3? Or C-1? When she finally found her way (by following all the cars), she luckily saw her hole captain, Paul, and latched onto him for dear life as he led the way to hole number three. Now she would just have to follow him out again, or she might have to spend the night in one of the hospitality tents.

This time, Momma listened. There were ropes to learn (literally)—crosswalk ropes and ropes from one green to the next tee box. If a player hit it in the *ruff*, the marshal might have to remove a stake or two or three to lower the rope—if requested by the player—and replace it with a hammer after the player had hit. *Seriously? A hammer?* Momma thought. Did they think she was a carpenter? The marshals were also warned not to hammer when someone was taking a shot—not even if it was a European.

And then there were the grandstand duties. The marshals were expected to rope off the stairs (those darn ropes again) and to turn spectators away if the grandstand was full. If they left for beer or the restroom, the marshal was to give them a little ticket with the hole number and time on it. The spectators had thirty minutes to return or the marshal was to deny them reentrance. God, what had Momma gotten herself into? Managing people was not her thing. She decided to avoid the grandstand at all costs.

The marshals were also to give people directions—to restrooms, to different holes, to concession stands, to hospitality tents, to the first aid station—the list went on and on. How could they be expected to *know* so much? By now, Momma was in a mild state of panic.

The Tournament

Despite her anxiety, Momma's first day on the job went pretty well. She chose the easiest job she could find—one that was practically foolproof—working the ropes to let spectators cross the fairway after players hit their drives. Pretty soon, Momma got the hang of it; in fact, she got a little cocky. She began confidently answering questions and giving directions, even though the only thing she knew for *sure* was where the restrooms were (having been there three times already that morning). She even started greeting people with her own motto, "Welcome to Minnesota," which was often met with strange looks since most people there were *from* Minnesota.

The next day—as expected, frankly—things got a little dicey. While idly standing by the green guarding the flagstick after the players had gone through (a position likely created just to keep her occupied), Momma glanced over at the (dreaded) grandstand and saw that it was almost full already! The afternoon grandstand team had not yet arrived, so she and her partner, Deb, sprang into action and took up their positions on each set of stairs. Then Momma pulled the rope across the entrance and turned over the sign to read FULL.

"Sorry," she informed the crowd. "We're full."

The only problem was that several people had left to buy food and drinks and now wanted reentry to rejoin their friends.

And who could blame them? At the same time, people (who were by now subject to the ticketing/timing process) were streaming *out* of the grandstand for one last drink/restroom run before the afternoon action. Not only was Momma writing tickets at warp speed, she also had to time people and (maybe, depending on their story) readmit some that had no tickets at all! Soon people were coming and going at such a dizzying pace that Momma's head was spinning.

Luckily, the grandstand team arrived in the nick of time and put things in order. Momma, near collapse, made her *own* run to the nearest wine tent.

On her final day of duty, Momma worked the tee box, where she was expected to operate the ropes (the ropes again!) so players could pass through and also keep the crowd quiet for their shots. Momma was bound and determined to do well, but she was racked with self-doubt.

Would she be able to undo (and tie up) the ropes at the right moment? What if she kept the players waiting? Tripped Rory? Even accidentally? Should she crouch down when players were shooting so others could see? Or should she raise her arms over her head in the universal "quiet" signal like they do on TV? Would she be *on* TV? Could she say anything to players, being an official marshal and all? She wasn't just a regular fan, after all. She totally forgot *what* she was, though, when she saw Bubba and cried out, "I love you, Bubba!" I'm sure Bubba's world is now complete.

By the time Momma came home that night, she was like a whipped pup, tired but happy. The Americans had pulled off the victory, and she had successfully masqueraded as a marshal. Here she is acting the part.

Momma and Deb on duty at the third green!

And here we are celebrating.

Lina, Deputy Marshal

WOOFDA!

USA!

37

OCTOBER

O ctober is one of my favorite months. It means that Momma's (Minnesota) golf season—including the revolving door of caregivers coming by and my endless trips to day care—are almost over. It also means that I get to celebrate my favorite holiday—Halloween!

Golf and Doggie Day Care

Although Momma also loves October (it *is* her birthday month, and she enjoys the gifts, attention, and so on), she will miss the endless tee times, shopping for golf outfits, and cocktails on the nineteenth hole that the end of the season brings. I, on the other paw, will be happy to see things return to normal here (a term I use loosely when woofing about life with Momma).

This year, Momma, in the vain hope of becoming a better doggie momma, and fearing a repeat of last year when the house flooded—with me at home gated in the bathroom—had decided that I could not stay at home by myself for several hours while she golfed. Therefore, she made up her mind—Momma would either find someone to "check on" (code for feed, walk, and play with) me, or she would take me to doggie day care.

Luckily, Momma was usually successful at finding a victim . . . er, *volunteer* to stop by. If not my personal favorite, Nanny Becky, she would enlist Bob, our next-door neighbor, or any other person in possession of our house key or garage code to stop by. Don't tell Momma—or our insurance company—that I woofed this, but I'm reasonably sure that Momma has lost track of who all *does* have access to our house, which sounds a little risky to me. Momma seems unconcerned, though ("Not to worry, Lina, I have that pet cam/surveillance system set up").

When schedules jibed, Momma would drop me off at doggie day care ("camp") on her way to the golf course. It is a top-notch facility with great care, but Momma has made it difficult for me to fit in there.

First, there was the tour she demanded before leaving me there for the first time and the inquisition about another "camper" in the small doggie play area (let's just say Momma has a lot to learn about being inclusive). And every time we go there, there's the embarrassing arrival. Momma—ostensibly to protect me from big dogs, but really to signal that I should have extra care—carries me in like a baby (causing many eye rolls among "camp counselors" and making me a laughingstock with the other dogs) along with my elephant toy (meant to sway staff and owners to the GOP) and a treat bag. She then hands me over to a weary counselor and instructs that after about two hours of play I should be placed in my cabin to rest—with the elephant!—and given my treats.

Her little production over, Momma finally dashes out the door for golf. She often forgets about me then, but sometimes checks the live web cam to check on me (she's paying for this, after all). If I am not immediately visible in the play area and it isn't my break time, Momma calls the camp and asks where I am. That practice came to a screeching halt one day, however, when, after Momma's incessant calling, she was informed that I had been placed in the air-conditioned doggie lounge up front where I would be more comfortable and they could give me a little more attention. ("Best just to let sleeping dogs lie, Lina.")

Even when she does see me in the small doggie play area, though, Momma can't help but interfere. If I am—for one minute—just sitting by myself, Momma has a "little chat" with camp counselors about my interaction (or lack thereof) with other dogs. "Lina doesn't seem to be very popular, does she?" or "Lina doesn't seem to be playing well with other dogs, does she?" Momma will inquire. To which a patient camp counselor will assure her, keeping his thoughts on who really has social issues to himself, that Lina is just fine.

The last time Momma dropped me off took the cake. Before releasing me to camp care, Momma always asks the counselor (in whose arms she is placing me) what his or her name is—the easier to ask for someone specific when she calls to check on me. This time, the girl's name was Candi. Momma, trying to bond quickly, said, "Oh, my gosh, that's my middle name!"

"Really?" asked Candi. "Candi or Candace?"

It was Candace, but Momma thought *Candy* would better cement the relationship, so she responded, "Candy."

"*Really?*" exclaimed Candi. "Do you spell it with an *i* or a *y*?"

At first, this stumped Momma because she did not know how to spell a name she really didn't have, but she quickly recovered and blurted out, "*Y*"—wouldn't that be the most common, after all?

"Oh," said a disappointed Candi. "Mine's with an *i*."

So much for bonding—although I'm sure Candi won't soon forget Candy.

The "October Surprise" and Halloween

Just when I thought we had settled in for the fall, I had a nice surprise—Momma went to Florida for more golf, and Dr. Becca and Winnie, her wiener dog, came to stay with me for a week. (Momma, gloating: "What a coincidence that both you and your friend, Hillary, had Weiner surprises in October, Lina!") We had a lot of fun, and the highlight of their stay was when Dr. Becca dressed us up in costumes and took us along to work on Halloween Day. Here we are—Winnie as

Wonder Woman and me as a princess ("Really going against type there," Momma sniped).

Winnie

Lina

I, for one, am looking forward to winter. Thank you, Dr. Becca and all my caregivers for the quality time you spent with me this season!

Lina, Camper and Princess

WOOFDA!

38

AN UBER THANKSGIVING

This year, Momma was invited to two Thanksgiving dinners. She was thrilled—that was at least one more invitation than she normally got. She happily looked forward to picking out an outfit, seeing good friends, sharing a glass of wine in front of a roaring fire, and partaking in a bountiful Thanksgiving meal (or two). Plus, now Momma could proudly respond, when asked, that yes, she had plans for Thanksgiving—in fact would be going to a nice restaurant with one group and later to the house of friends in Eagan. She eagerly accepted both invitations.

The trouble with Momma, though, is that she really can't handle two social engagements in one day (she is just not good at mingling and is frankly getting a little long in the canines, and she knew it). Nevertheless, she was so excited about the idea of two festive gatherings that she figured (à la Scarlett O'Hara in *Gone with the Wind*) that she would think about the details tomorrow.

Well, tomorrow (yesterday now) finally came, and she was forced to figure out the logistics of Thanksgiving Day. She would still be social and perky at the first dinner, but she was worried about the second one later in the after-noon—she knew in her heart of hearts that she would be too full and tired to stay and visit very long. (Leaving wouldn't really be a problem, though, Momma rationalized. She would just use her trusty, timeworn—and totally bogus "I've got to get home to Lina" excuse.) Anyway, since Momma was riding with a friend, she decided that she had to figure out an early ride home.

That's when inspiration struck. She would use Uber! (She had recently heard Uncle Chuck use the term as a verb—"I will have to Uber it to the airport," and it sounded so cool that she wanted to be able to say that she, too, had Ubered it somewhere—anywhere.)

This, then, would fit in perfectly with her Thanksgiving Day plan—she could attend both gatherings, socialize a little at the second, maybe grab some dessert (and another glass of wine), and then tell everyone smugly that she had to leave—she was Ubering it home. Momma eagerly loaded the app onto her phone.

There, she thought, *I'm set—just tap and go as they say.*

It turned out she wasn't "set," though, because she immediately got an email welcoming her to Uber and urging her to "get started" and sign up for a ride and create an account! This threw her, of course. She didn't want to sign up for a ride— not *now*, anyway, and she thought she had already created an account. Nevertheless, she stumbled through the process and created an account (maybe for a second time—did she now possibly have two accounts?), trying to put the whole thing to bed so she could move on to more important details like planning what she would wear that day.

Then she got a pop-up question—did she want Uber to know her location? Well, of course they had to know her location to pick her up for a ride, but did they need her location *now*? Needless to say, she was baffled—and not just a little frustrated—and clicked on the little *x*, which made the question go away—at least for the time being.

Then Momma got another email—this time informing her that she hadn't completed her payment information. She navigated the maze that led back into her account (she thought) and keyed in one of her credit card numbers, the expiration date, and the secret code on the back. *There*, she thought. *Done.*

Thanksgiving Day was pleasant. She enjoyed the camaraderie with friends and a dinner with all the trimmings, and soon it was time to say good-bye and head to Erik and Cheryl's house. Momma's energy was already flagging, but she was bound and determined to be a good guest and join in the festivities.

Secretly, though, she was already planning how she could gracefully leave early by using the doggie excuse. After visiting for a short time and nibbling on some chocolates, Momma decided it was time to go. She was ready to dial up (so to woof) Uber on her phone.

Because she was not too sure about what she was doing (and hoped to avoid making a fool of herself), she slipped away to the foyer and surreptitiously tapped on the Uber icon. Momma immediately got a prompt asking her "Where to?" Relieved that she knew the answer to that one (she *did* know her home address, after all), she quickly typed it in. Next she learned that she had to pick out a type of car—options ranged from an X to an SUV model. Quickly settling on the cheapest one, Momma chose the model X (not to be confused with a Model T, Momma—just woofing).

Anyway, she thought she was on the right track because the phone screen suddenly showed a line moving from her current location to her home. The app also indicated that the car would be there in about half an hour. *Fine*, Momma thought. Maybe there was time for one more snack, and then she would snappily announce that she was going to Uber it home and take her leave.

As with most things Momma, however, things did not go as planned. Soon she noticed that the arrival time of the car kept changing; then she got a message that no cars were available at all. At this point, she was not sure that she had done the model X request thing right. Was the car really late, or wasn't there a car coming at all? Should she keep checking the app, or would she have to embarrass herself and ask for a ride home? At this point, people were also wondering what she had been doing on her phone for the last half hour.

Momma, in a mild panic by now, decided that she needed help. She quietly asked some young people (who were undoubtedly familiar with Uber) if they knew what was happening. After a brief view of her phone, the hip, young smart alecks informed her that, no, a car was *not* coming. It was Thanksgiving, after all, they patiently explained to her, and a lot of people probably needed a ride home.

Luckily, a friend (who Momma was pretty sure did not want to leave the party just yet) kindly offered her a ride home. Momma still wasn't convinced that the model X wasn't coming for her, though, so she—trying to sound all upbeat—trilled out that she had called (*called?*) Uber and that they might be showing up, so please tell them that she had already left.

Today, Momma got another email from Uber informing her that her account is still missing payment information. I think she has given up. ("Lina, I think I'll just use Yellow Cab from now on—at least they know how to run a business.")

Lina, Still Waiting for My Thanksgiving Dinner

WOOFDA!

39

PARTING WOOFS

Shortly after Momma took possession of me, I began to suspect that my life as a dog was, to put it mildly, not typical. She had good intentions but totally lacked in doggie parenting skills and common sense. Nevertheless, we somehow stumbled through the first two years and—despite all the calamities and against all odds—are still standing.

Where has the time gone? Well, a lot of it was spent at myriad vet offices, specialty clinics, and hospitals in Minni and Florida. How much of the time at the vet was due to Momma's inability to deal with minor—or even nonexistent—health issues on her own and how much was due to her desire to visit a hunky doc (unnecessarily . . . again) is anyone's guess.

A good chunk of the time has also been spent on water in Momma's endless quest to make me a swimmer. It's not going to happen, but that doesn't stop her from placing me on anything that floats (including a noodle in her friend Debbie's pool this summer) and paddling around in the water. And, by the way, just how was it that I—a water-hating dog—ended up living in the "Land of 10,000 Lakes" and on one of the Ten Thousand Islands of Florida?

Thankfully—when I wasn't being examined by a vet or being held hostage on a body of water—I got to enjoy long playdates with my BFFs Gracie, CoCoa and Winnie! I also got to spend gobs of time with Gracie's family in Florida. In fact, I think they view me as their very own rescue dog. I'm just woofing . . .

And, of course, I got to spend quality time with Nanny Becky and Dr. Becca. I know I will always have my safe and special space with them—which is important because you never know how this Trump thing is going to turn out. How does he stand on doggie rights, I wonder? Also, I'm Australian, and I live in fear that Momma does not have my proper documentation on hand. In any event, I am thinking about turning our house into a sanctuary site—just in case.

Momma and I have managed to settle into the rhythm of a daily routine, but I never let my guard (dog) down. One never knows when disaster (or at least another supremely embarrassing Momma moment) will take place. One thing that I know for sure—as long as Momma and I are together, I'll never be at a loss for woofs!

So despite the fact that *Lina Unleashed* is drawing to a close, I'm not going to be all coy about it—there will be a sequel. How could there not be? I have many more years with Momma and many more tails to tell.

Please don't forget to check out the ongoing action at linasdogblog.com!

Lina, Survivor and Snowflake!

WOOFDA!

To be continued . . .

ABOUT THE AUTHOR

Lina, whose nom de *paw*lume is Little Big Ears, is a two-year-old Toy Australian Shepherd who hails from Florida. She is an acclaimed blogger and a keen observer of human behavior. She is the proud recipient of the 2015 Pawlitzer for her work on linasdogblog.com.

When Lina is not busy writing, she enjoys chasing her big orange ball, chewing on a bully stick, performing tricks and playing with her furry friends. She does not enjoy being in any lake, river, stream, ocean, or even the rain.

Lina and her human, Robin Kelleher, divide their time between Minnesota—the Land of 10,000 Lakes—and the Ten Thousand Islands of Florida.